# PRAISE FOR JOHN STERLING

"John is one of the most interesting and unique people I know. He is an authentic and creative leader whose passion inspires. John knows how to build and motivate teams to success. I've learned many things from John about sales and sales teams, but the most important thing I learned was how to serve as a genuine leader. John has a unique ability to see the potential in people and make them feel like they can conquer the world. I've been inspired by John in our years together at Datastream, and I'm still inspired by him today."

 **—Scott Millwood**
 Founder and CEO, Yesflow

"John hit a homerun early by most people's definition. He grew a business from start-up to publicly-traded to sold, all while quite young. It wasn't luck; it was hard work and the school of hard knocks. He's subsequently taken his skillset (as he says, 'my 10,000 hours') and has begun to 'give back.' John helps various stage start-ups and ongoing concerns that are 'stuck' get 'unstuck.' He brings immediate, tangible advice that adds real value. Not just 'paint it red' advice; his advice is actionable 'here's how AND here's why' advice. Furthermore, he brings HIS paintbrush and painters along when necessary. John is a seasoned coach that adds value immediately, and I recommend him."

 **—Bill Garcia**
 Co-Founder and Managing Partner, TableForce

"I worked with/for John Sterling for my first 10 years right out of college. I walked into a booming technology world (in the mid-to-late '90s) with very little background in the technology space. John created an environment that fostered self-improvement and self confidence among his team, along with a sales process that, if followed, almost guaranteed individual and team success. He's an inspirational leader who is passionate about helping people meet their personal goals. He strips away the complexity and keeps the team focused on the overall mission. I will always consider John to be my first mentor, and still consult with him on a regular basis 20-plus years since the day I first met him."

—**Tap Haley**
Chief Sales Officer, Yesflow

"Big John has been a great influence in my life, professionally and personally. 'Whatever you are, be a great one!' is the message he shared with me fresh from The Citadel, and it's something that I try to embrace selling for SAP and with my family and friends each day."

—**Nathan Barr**
Vice President, Sales, SAP

"John Sterling is a leader. That's the best way to describe him. He's a sales leader with an amazing track record of designing and implementing revenue-producing strategies for companies large and small. He's also a community and state leader as he works with organizations like NEXT and Clemson University to build a stronger start-up ecosystem in his hometown of Greenville, South Carolina, and with The Honor Foundation to make the area a welcoming location for retiring Navy SEAL's and Special Operations veterans. John is one of my 'go-to' contacts when action and results are needed."

—**John Moore**
Venture Partner, Material Capital Partners

"I worked for John for a few years, and I can honestly say I learned more about sales from him than any other manager in my career. He is always looking for a 'win-win' for any client, and taught me and many others that skill. He is a master motivator; time spent with him will make you a better person. I only wish I could have worked with him longer."

—**Linton "Bubba" West**
Associate Broker, Sea Island Company

"When I moved to Greenville, John Sterling's name came up again and again as someone you 'have' to know, not only as a business associate but as a mentor and friend. John's ability to find the time and desire to see others succeed is unwavering. He understands that collaboration is at the heart of good relationships and is quick to lend a kind word, direction, or thoughts to any issue you might have. His desire to see others fulfill their dreams can only be connected to someone who is fulfilling theirs daily. One of the greatest things about John is his desire to learn. He's not one who believes he's seen it all, done it all, or learned it all. He freely asks what others think about an issue, not because someone taught him to do that, but because he genuinely desires input coming from an angle he might have overlooked. This isn't something you often see in a person as successful as John."

—**James Vogt**

Director of Sales, New South Construction Supply & Former EODCS, SEAL Team Six, US Navy.

# SALES

# FOR

# NOOBS

*What if sales could be a high-income, high-security*
*dream job in two years (or fewer)?*

# SALES
# for
# NOOBS

Everything Sales Rookies
Need to Know to Crush Quota,
Get Promoted, and Kick A$$

## John Sterling

Terrier Holdings LLC
Greenville, SC

This book is for informational purposes only. It is not intended to provide professional advice or to address all circumstances that might arise. Individuals and entities using this document are encouraged to consult their own counsel. The author and publisher specifically disclaim any and all liability arising directly or indirectly from the use of any information contained in this book.

The conversations in this book are based on the author's recollections, though they are not intended to represent word-for-word transcripts. Rather, the author has retold them in a way that communicates the meaning of what was said. In the author's humble opinion, the essence of the dialogue is accurate in all instances.

*Sales for Noobs* copyright © 2020 by John Sterling

Terrier Holdings LLC
Greenville, SC
www.SchoolForNoobs.com
Send feedback to John@SchoolForNoobs.com

Printed in the United States of America

Publisher's Cataloging-In-Publication Data

    Names: Sterling, John (John Maxwell), 1961- author.
    Title: Sales for noobs : everything sales rookies need to know to crush quota,
       get promoted, and kick a$$ / John Sterling.
    Description: Greenville, South Carolina : Terrier Holdings LLC, [2021] |
       Includes bibliographical references.
    Identifiers: ISBN 9781735925301 (paperback) | ISBN 9781735925318
       (hardback) | ISBN 9781735925325 (ebook)
    Subjects: LCSH: Sales personnel. | Selling. | Success in business.
    Classification: LCC HF5439.5 .S74 2021 (print) | LCC HF5439.5 (ebook) |
       DDC 658.85--dc23

*This first book of mine is dedicated to the hundreds of college grads who chose me and my company for their first sales job. I really didn't know that much about sales when I started (like most salespeople) so together, we figured out systems, processes, and attitudes that worked in our field. At the beginning, I can remember having to get permission from some of the parents when we wanted these potential superstars to travel overseas, particularly in Asia!*

*We were fortunate in that we were able to select the best available sales candidates from several great schools close to our HQ and we became, at least for a time, an extension of what they were doing in frats and sororities, etc. (at least some of it).*

*It's been over 10 years since we sold that company, and not a day goes by that I don't talk to or communicate with at least one of the old sales crew. As you will see in the book, many have gone on to continued greatness as high earning sales people, sales managers, CEOs and company founders. Sales is one of the best ways to get started in business—everyone's in sales even if it doesn't say that on the org chart.*

*Last but not least, our founder Larry Blackwell deserves a big shout out. Larry was a Navy Officer and an Engineer with a PhD. Larry poked and prodded us along, particularly me, to write everything down and create repeatable processes instead of "winging it." He also built a helluva company.*

*I hope you enjoy the book and will check out my website if you want to dig deeper on some of these ideas.*

# GO BEYOND THE BOOK.

Let's continue your training. Additional resources await you at www. SchoolForNoobs.com.

You'll learn to make prospects take you seriously, sell high-ticket products and services with ease, and get paid a helluva lot more than you ever imagined in your dreams.

# CONTENTS

# CHAPTER 1

# SO, YOU'VE SUDDENLY BECOME A SALESPERSON

"**W**hat have I gotten myself into?"

Just about every salesperson in history has asked themselves this question, usually shortly after beginning their first sales job. If you're asking this question now, you're not alone. And you've got the right book to help you.

Since you're reading this book, I suspect you're just starting your sales journey. If I had to bet, I'd say sales is not your first choice. You probably didn't even go to school for sales. But like most salespeople I've met, the career path to the job you wanted no longer exists or you changed your mind somewhere along the way.

And now you're in sales. And you're trying to figure out how on earth to make it work.

At the time of this writing, the coronavirus pandemic shutdown has killed around 40 percent of businesses in the United States alone.[1] The

---

1 "Study: 40% of Businesses Fail to Reopen after a Disaster," Access, accessed October 31, 2020, https://www.accesscorp.com/access-in-the-news/study-40-percent-businesses-fail-reopen-disaster.

surviving employees have had to scramble to find work. Many have turned to sales, just as they did following the economic recessions in 2000 and 2008. This is not a surprise, as sales jobs account for more than half of all the "recession-proof" work available.[2] No matter what's happening in the stock market or at hospitals, companies will continue to have problems to solve, and business owners will always be happy to pay salespeople to find and deliver them money.

Look at sales potential this way. Imagine you own a business and can pay a new salesperson 10 percent of the money/gross profit they bring you. That's net new money you weren't pulling in before. Say that salesperson brings you a million dollars in 2021. You're happy to pay them $100,000 and pocket the other $900,000, right? This is why sales jobs don't disappear even when the market gets rough.

Your hourly wages or salary probably covers all (or most) of your living expenses. If you're any good at sales, the commission on top is a nice extra. You probably imagine one day you'll get a "real" job, but for now, sales is an opportunity to earn some money and get your foot in the door.

Many young people go into sales because they think they're not qualified for other professions, or because they assume there's no other way to get into business. It's hard to get hired as an architect with no architecture degree, but unqualified hiring happens every day in sales.

However it is you wound up in sales, you've realized one hard truth by now: Selling isn't easy.

Trying to convince strangers to give you their money is one of the most complex jobs out there. During your sales training, you learned you had to use specific keywords, position your posture a certain way, negotiate like this, or corner the customer like that.

But nine times out of ten, what do you sell? Nada. Meteorologists have better luck at their jobs, and weather forecasting is fortune-telling for people in suits.

---

2    Grant Cardone, "Sales Jobs at Top or Recession-Proof Jobs," HuffPost, updated December 6, 2017, https://www.huffpost.com/entry/sales-jobs-at-top-or-rece_b_378674.

As a sales noob, you're a fish in a shark tank. Your job probably feels like a constant battle to defend your product against customer objections, competitor attacks, and demands for special discounts. It's exhausting. Even if you say and do all the things you were taught, you may still get eaten for lunch by three evil little words:

"Not right now."

So, you're stuck. And any time we're stuck on a challenge, we go looking for help. You've probably asked Grandpa, Google, and the person who's been around the business awhile and knows the ropes. On your quest to close, you've looked up advice from experts. *Sales for Noobs* probably isn't the first sales book you've read, but it should have been. Don't get me wrong, there's a ton of good sales information out there.

But noobs should start with the basics, not the advanced stuff. You need a foundation before you learn the complicated tricks.

# COULD SALES BE THE SHORTCUT TO YOUR DREAM JOB?

Before I tell you how this book will help you make it big in sales, it's worth pointing out that this profession, often viewed as a last resort, is really a golden opportunity. If you're starting your career in sales instead of your dream position in a field associated with your college major, don't despair. Celebrate! You're one of the lucky ones—if you learn to lean into this experience, that is.

The majority of people who start their careers in sales go on to run their own businesses and often become CEOs. Most business owners in North America began in sales. In fact, many billionaire entrepreneurs, such as the Dallas Mavericks owner Mark Cuban and former Starbucks CEO Howard Schultz, began their careers in sales. Sales is one of the most interesting and mysterious games in the world.

And I've packed the most useful lessons from my career into this book to help you get off to a great start. You've got the guide you need right here in your hands.

Think of *Sales for Noobs* as your secret playbook. It shows you what to do and, more importantly, who to be in every conversation with potential customers and in your day-to-day sales routine. What you learn from this book will work for you regardless of whether you decide to stay in sales or go on to a different job. Let me explain why I can promise you this with confidence.

# WHAT THIS BOOK IS (NOT) ABOUT

Did you read the magazine *Highlights for Children* when you were a kid? My favorite activity was the hidden picture puzzle. *Find the golf club, horseshoe, and balloon in this picture of a carnival.* Hours and hours of fun. (Ugh, this was before the Internet.)

Each monthly issue also featured a two-panel *Goofus and Gallant* cartoon. The left panel always showed Goofus acting selfish and rude, an example of how *not* to be a good kid. The right panel always showed Gallant, a little boy who was kind and respectful. The editor of *Highlights* once explained the purpose of the short comic: Without Goofus, Gallant would be bland, and no one would pay attention.

Kids see parts of themselves in both characters. No one is as good as Gallant, and no one is as bad as Goofus. Being more like Gallant is something to strive for.[3]

Other sales authors write books that claim to show you how to be a Gallant salesperson. They tell you exactly what to say and do—"use this script, memorize this psychological trick, call 100 prospects a day." It's a big to-do list. That's a lot for anyone to remember.

I wouldn't have written this book if the existing library of sales books set sales noobs up for success. When several of my former employees

---

3    Eric Zorn, "Goofus, Gallant—the Inside Story," Chicago Tribune, June 14, 2006, https://blogs.chicagotribune.com/news_columnists_ezorn/2006/06/goofus_gal-lantt.html.

(who went on to become multimillionaires through sales) asked me to write a sales book, I knew what not to write: another do-this-and-the-sale-will-magically-happen Gallant book. Without a Goofus, Gallant is bland and (like most sales books) not very helpful.

*Sales for Noobs* is a Goofus book. Unlike every other sales book, it tells you explicitly what *not* to do.

How *not* to prospect.

What *not* to say during a sales call.

Which sales jobs and promotions to *never* accept.

How *not* to hire and train salespeople when you're a manager.

By showing you what *not* to do, this book can help new salespeople avoid flawed advice from well-meaning sales gurus.

You've probably heard of billionaire investor Warren Buffett. But do you know his partner, Charlie Munger? Munger is known for snippy proverbs called Mungerisms, one of which expresses why I took an unusual approach with this book:

"You don't have to pee on an electric fence to learn not to do it."[4]

That's what this book is about. What derails a sale—and eventually a salesperson's career—is *not* that they forget to do what they were trained to do. It's that they do what they should *never* do, because nobody ever told them not to!

I've made idiotic mistakes myself and watched plenty of other salespeople blow it. Take away these mishaps, and you're virtually guaranteed to succeed in sales.

Add to the confusion the list of self-destructive beliefs many sales noobs have that just aren't true. It's all head trash. The wrong way salespeople dress, carry themselves, handle objections, negotiate, and schedule their day brings their chances of making the sale close to zero. But get all this right early in your sales job, and you'll make a lot more money, have more fun, and build a rewarding career in sales (if you choose).

Fortunately, going from noob to pro doesn't have to be figured out from scratch!

---

4   Gautam Baid, The Joys of Compounding: The Passionate Pursuit of Lifelong Learning (New York: Columbia Press, 2020), 340.

All the Goofus advice you're about to read comes from the careers of more than 144 salespeople I've had the pleasure of working with for over 20 years. Many became millionaires either through sales or entrepreneurship, which is really just sales with a fancier name. In preparation for this book, I asked them directly, "What do you wish you would have known earlier in your sales career?" Every answer started with an impassioned, "If only I'd known to *never* . . ." They described ways they tried to pitch products, meet with prospects, or prep their weekly schedules that, in retrospect, drove would-be customers away. Many also regret choosing the wrong sales job.

For example, one sales executive who loves sports sold legal services to businesses for years. He hated it. He, like all my interviewed sales experts, "noobed" himself without realizing it. These mistakes are the ingredients to your success recipe. Learn how not to noob yourself and you'll figure out your path to success faster, earn bigger commissions, and make something of yourself.

There are no long-winded theories here. You'll be able to use these tips right away. I wrote this book to simplify sales. Specifically, I want to help you get the best start you can. In a complicated world, simplification has value.

Years ago, I was listening to a Tony Robbins motivational CD. On the topic of goals, he said, "Stop right now and take one quick action on each of your goals." At the time, I had one-day-itis. I wanted to own my dream home on the golf course. Had I run the numbers? No. Not until that moment with Tony. I paused the CD and forced myself to do the exercise.

I figured it would take years, but when I met with my personal banker, I realized I was closer than I thought. After I met with my real estate broker and saw the prices on available properties, I figured out that I could do it. Within three months, I accomplished my goal. All because I took action right away.

I look back at these simple moments with gratitude because they change everything. My imagination told me a house on a golf course must be out of reach. Reality was different. This is often the case, especially when you are starting out. But truthfully, breaking through your limitations is a lifelong challenge. There is nothing I want more for you than to create the breakthroughs for yourself.

Along with the derailing mistakes salespeople often make, you'll learn what self-made millionaires did early in their careers to succeed. This will reduce your trial and error. In an economic downturn, do you really have time to waste? The advice in this book worked amid the chaos of Y2K in 2000, during the 2002 dot-com bubble burst, the 2008 recession, and the 2020 coronavirus pandemic.

You'll learn what's changed through the years in the sales game and what hasn't. For example, COVID-19 has shifted the majority of businesses online versus in-person. Before the pandemic, prospects wanted you to meet them at their office face-to-face. Now, video calls are the norm and in-person visits are the exception.

You're going to start by building a foundation of success for year-one in sales and beyond. How well you build your foundation will have a 10x multiplier on your future earning power. Yes, you could figure out the advice in this book over a lifetime of experimentation like the rest of us. But with some purposeful planning, you can get a head start. Wouldn't you like to boost your earning power now and avoid embarrassing mistakes?

Every salesperson I've seen implement the advice in this book became successful over the long haul. It's important to keep the big picture in view. You will see a difference as soon as you apply my advice, but this isn't a sell-more-quick book. Remember the big picture. Salespeople tend to get carried away with results when the focus should be on the whole process, not just the result.

Your sales numbers will go up and down throughout your sales journey. Just like in life, don't ruminate over short-term failures. You're playing year-one of a career that will span decades. If you keep improving, maintain your discipline, and focus on trading value for money, you will succeed.

Play it cool, Luke.

# WHO IS JOHN STERLING?

Before we go any further, you should know a little about your sales mentor.

I earned my political science degree (thought I wanted to be a lawyer) from the Citadel in Charleston, South Carolina. I put in 10,000 hours of reviewing, optimizing, and running sales teams early in my career. I started as an entry-level salesperson and stuck with it long enough to become an account manager, then a sales manager, then a vice president. As VP of sales, I grew the company Datastream from a team of four to one-thousand-plus employees and helped take the company public.

In 2006, we sold Datastream to Infor for $200 million.

At Datastream, I managed more than 100 sales reps globally and reached $120 million in revenue. I also led five international acquisitions and managed sales offices in the United States, Germany, France, the United Kingdom, the Netherlands, Argentina, Australia, Singapore, and China. That sounds like a lot if you're a noob. And it was a lot. But most of the international work came after 15 years of incremental improvements, which prepared me/us for those kinds of challenges. My 20-year global sales career was made possible by a great start in sales with lots and lots of practice and at-bats with customers and prospects.

Sell well and sell a lot, over a stretch of time, and you can do just about anything you want in life.

After exiting Datastream, I started helping business owners ramp up revenue. I created a sales rookie mentoring service. I developed outstanding software tools that help companies and rookies improve their sales performance. You can find those at SchoolForNoobs.com.

Over the years, I've learned from some of the best sales trainers out there. You'll find their ideas throughout this book, but without their $10,000 training fees! These influencers include Zig Ziglar, my first sales trainer; Bill Lee, the man who showed me how to hire to a specific profile that matched the type of person that was proven to do well on my sales team; Bill Garcia, who taught me (and our entire global sales force) how to negotiate; and Al Ries, who taught me to focus on qualified prospects in a small niche, not "anyone who might need this product."

I wish I'd received their sales education earlier in my career. I'd be even farther than I am. But you can learn it all right now, at the start of your sales journey. You'll learn everything I wish I'd known.

## THIS BOOK WILL WORK FOR YOU

If your product doesn't have satisfied customer testimonials, you shouldn't be selling it. Books are no different. So let me introduce some salespeople I've worked with over the years who, by following my counsel, made big money in sales.

They come from different backgrounds, have wildly different personalities, and currently work in different fields, although many stayed in high-tech selling. My advice worked for them, and it will work for you.

## EVEN IF YOU'RE SELLING TO BIG CUSTOMERS

When I hired John Harrison, he'd just graduated from college and was teaching and coaching football and basketball at Berkeley High School. He'd had a stellar college baseball career but no business experience at all. Sales was his first real job, and his new salary paid double the coaching position.

One account John worked on was the Miami, Florida, Fire Department. He went in, met patiently with the fire chief, and closed a relatively small deal. One conversation led to another, and John booked a face-to-face meeting with the mayor of Miami. John made a compelling offer, did a ton of work, and built a solid rapport. The mayor said yes to using our software product in every city department, not just fire and rescue. The monster deal added up to $25 million, the first of many multimillion-dollar enterprise sales John made, collectively earning himself millions in commissions.

This marquee account taught John to think not just about the sale in front of him, but about every additional sale that can happen through one account. Most salespeople deal with a local or lower-level decision maker and don't even think about stepping up to the big leagues. John did. He got comfortable with large opportunities worth millions, and so can you.

In fact, I've learned that talking to the CEO of a Fortune 500 corporation is much easier than selling to a middle manager at regional headquarters. How do you get your foot in the door at companies with massive budgets? I'll show you, just like I showed John.

## EVEN IF SALES IS YOUR FIRST JOB

Just like John Harrison, Crystal Novella's first real job was sales. I also hired her right out of college, and noticed she had a knack for seeking out big prospects. One of her targets was the United States Postal Service. This young woman stuck with it for over three years. In the end, the deal she closed was worth $10 million. Her diligent approach led her to land even bigger accounts down the road.

I'll never forget how different that big figure looked for Crystal and me relative to the USPS. I asked the local newspaper to come take pictures of the contract signing. "Software company inks $10 million deal with the Postal Service!" But the value of money is relative. The deal was a drop in the bucket to the USPS. For them, spending a few million with us was like me buying a stamp. Crystal learned this perspective early and has continued closing big deals. She's become a patient powerhouse.

So can you, even if sales is your first job.

## EVEN IF YOU'RE YOUNG

Nate Barr was 21 years old when I hired him. He had just graduated as a senior private, the lowest possible rank as a graduating senior from the Citadel, same as I did. He did everything I asked him to do—everything you'll learn in this book—and stuck with it. His first couple of years were just okay, nothing to write home about, but he kept following the rules.

Then he sold Georgia Pacific on a $13 million deal. The 8 percent commission made him a millionaire.

Nate's biggest deal to-date is $40 million. He's a sales manager for SAP now, and he started in sales like most of you will.

It took Nate (and just about everyone) a few years of focusing on the basics to get good at sales. Winning big in this game takes time. The sooner you read this book, the faster you'll compress the time required to succeed. You can go into a sales organization without a plan, work for a bad manager, and slosh around till you're 30 years old. Or you can get your act together like Nate and start developing a skill set for long-term success in your early twenties.

Your call.

## EVEN IF YOU WANT TO TRAVEL

TJ Pomian is another Citadel graduate I hired right out of school. He was a sharp young man eager to tackle international sales. He got a competing job offer when we hired him from somewhere else offering more money, but we promised to get him selling internationally as soon as possible. Within a couple of years, he was doing well as an inside salesperson.

Then he had an opportunity to work with De Beers South Africa, the world's largest diamond mine. He closed the deal, which began his stellar international sales career. He relocated to South Africa and built up that region, then expanded into the Middle East.

TJ showed up eager and ready to work. He was the first to ask, "What do we need to do?" I always tell sales managers that if you can hire enough TJs, you can take any hill or dominate any market. Even when he was taking inside sales calls from his tiny half-cubicle, there was no question TJ would succeed as an outside salesperson and manager.

After that first job, TJ was called up by the Army. He went on to serve two tours of duty in Afghanistan, reached the rank of colonel in the National Guard where he still serves, and then became a Sales Manager at Oracle. He is now a Sales Manager for SalesForce.com. This is probably one of the best arcs a young professional could ever hope for. And it all started when he crushed the duties required to succeed in his first job, including picking the company best situated to help him fulfill his goals.

## EVEN IF YOU DON'T WANT TO STAY IN SALES

Every sales noob should aspire to be the next Reed Wilson. After graduating from the Citadel, Reed came to work for me in inside sales. He followed the plan, did what he was supposed to do, and, after a few years, earned a position in outside sales—and an appointment with Dell, the multibillion-dollar computer company. He closed the deal, which involved all of the Dell manufacturing facilities around the world.

Reed rolled his success and what he learned from the deal into starting his own business, which today helps over 150 companies manage and outsource IT. Reed has built a great business, and it all started with his outstanding success during the first few years in inside sales.

It takes expertise and time to be like Reed. You have to know what you're doing. Follow this book, and you will.

## EVEN IF YOUR PROSPECTS HAVE A DIFFERENT BACKGROUND

Want to lose an international deal in one sentence? Say this: "Well, back in the United States, we don't do it that way."

Once you get past local customs, people are people. Selling is selling. What works to close a deal in China works in England, whether you're selling cell phones or enterprise software. I can tell you from experience it's the same. You need to know what your prospect wants, and they need to know the price.

Years ago, I was in Singapore sitting with a Chinese man and an 80-year-old Taiwanese woman, the two owners of a business we were trying to purchase. On the long flight from the US to Asia, I had read up on how Americans should do business in Asia. When I greeted my prospects, I used the respectful small talk I memorized on the plane. I may have even bowed a little!

"Mr. Sterling," the woman said, "if you don't mind, just get to the point. I'm 80 years old. I measure my time in months and weeks, not years."

A huge chunk of international selling is learning to be yourself and following your process. I'll teach you what that looks like.

## EVEN IF YOU CHANGE INDUSTRIES

I've been able to take people fresh out of university from diverse backgrounds and help them become multimillion-dollar dealmakers in software, manufacturing equipment sales, industrial maintenance services, oil pipelines, refineries, and more. Learn to sell well, and you can sell anything to anyone in any business.

Former college volleyball player Jennie Shaw worked with me selling software. Her goal was to make $400,000 in one year and sell internationally. She has an extremely extroverted personality, but our work environment was an office, not an outside adventure. Our company wasn't the right fit for her dreams, so she changed jobs after a few years of doing very well in inside sales. Her new company, a medical implant device company based in Sweden, empowered her to flourish.

Today, she's head of sales for a company that sells to reconstructive surgeons. All the while, she gets to travel for work to beautiful European countries like Sweden. Jennie knew exactly what she wanted, and her time with us helped her get it. For her, that meant leaving to find a better match.

This book will help you find your optimal match, too.

# EVEN IF YOU'RE STILL IN COLLEGE

John Byrum (JB) interned for me while he was in school at Furman University in Greenville, South Carolina. He started as a low-paid intern for the first summer. During his second summer internship, he learned more about processing leads and how the sales cycle worked. Before the second summer was over, we had made him a full-time offer. He accepted.

We had a proven commodity lined up to start in sales in a year, and JB had lined up a job he felt very good about. During his senior year, he already had his job locked up while the majority of his classmates were scrambling to find anyone to give them a break. The earlier you can start in sales, the better. Over time, JB earned several promotions. First, from intern to inside sales specialist, then sales manager, then VP of Sales.

If you're just beginning and want to follow JB's path, an ideal progression would be to start selling something part-time as soon as possible. Sell anything that starts the clock ticking on your cumulative experience in sales.

After 10 years, JB started his own wine importing business. He's started and sold three more companies since then. He's a multimillionaire today because he developed his skills early.

Have you noticed all these stories involve taking on brand new salespeople? If I found somebody who was three or four years into their career, I almost never hired them. Because at that point, they've usually turned bad thinking and bad selling techniques into habits.

That may sound like bad news if you've been in sales for a while. But there's a caveat here.

# EVEN IF YOU'VE ALREADY HAD SALES TRAINING

What you glean from this book will work, even if you've been in the game for a while and have received sales training. Or perhaps I should say, this book will prepare you in spite of your training!

The advice in this book worked when I hired Landy Wingard. I had to completely retrain him. His previous employer, a Fortune 500

telecommunications company, taught him to do things that an effective salesperson should *never* do. Only after we broke those bad habits did he go on to become a sales success. Landy and I laugh about it today, the fact that we almost didn't hire him. He's gone on to be a crusher salesperson and wrote a pretty good book about selling, to boot.

## EVEN IF YOU'RE NOT A SMOOTH TALKER

Sales is often perceived as trying to fast-talk people into buying whatever garbage you're selling. In reality, selling is having an honest conversation to figure out if the prospect needs what you're selling.

Several years ago, I went into a Best Buy for a new TV. It was the morning of Super Bowl Sunday, my brother-in-law had come into town for the big game, and my old television had died right on Super Bowl Sunday. My brother-in-law and I went into the store together, and a Best Buy customer salesperson walked up to us.

"Hey, big guy," he said to me. "What'd you come in for today?"

"Good question," I said. "We're here for a new TV."

"OK. Let's go back to the TVs." As we walked together, he asked us some questions.

"Why are you coming in for a TV?" "What kind of TV are you looking for?" "When do you need the TV?"

"What size space do you have for this TV?" "What's your budget?"

By the time we got back to the TV section, he'd worked out exactly what I wanted. I had 800 bucks in my pocket, and I needed a TV immediately to watch the Super Bowl in crystal clarity.

"All right. Just follow me. We'll get what you want."

No sales spiel. No "persuasion." No bullshit. After he helped us pick out the perfect TV, I offered him a job, and he took it. He succeeded because he proved he didn't have to be a schmoozer to sell. That's what sets successful salespeople apart from the not-so-successful ones.

A few years later, I met with an oil executive in Denmark. To open the conversation, I simply asked him, "Can you tell me what the situation is?"

He looked shocked. "No one—no one has ever asked me that before."

I made the sale. No beating around the bush. Just asking people straight what they need.

Amazing how a simple sales lesson from Greenville, South Carolina, works in Denmark!

## EVEN IF YOU'D RATHER START YOUR OWN BUSINESS

Reed Wilson isn't the only salesperson I hired who became an entrepreneur. Another sales guy, Parker Smith, had an IQ so high I almost didn't hire him because he was outside our typical hiring profile (the too-smart rule).

Fortunately, he had both smarts and hunger. He killed it in sales, then left to start what is now the biggest destination golf company in Myrtle Beach, South Carolina.

## ... If You Commit for Two Years

Every millionaire sales professional I know took a few years to get there. The range in my experience has been 10 years minimum, with 20 being the sweet spot of success. The millions may not start rolling in year one, but the process becomes clear. Throw away the bad habits and start doing what works, like getting to work on time, making the number of calls you must make every day, framing the world in your favor, under- standing what your prospects are going through, and learning about the problem you're solving.

Do all this beginning in year one, and by the end of year two, you're going to be the top dog. Or you can be a Goofus in year one, blame your crappy results on being new, and noob yourself. It's true that the first year is never the best because you're learning.

You're probably in new territory. You don't have rapport with customers or momentum with prospects. But don't let any disappointing year one numbers fool you. If you're following the right process and working in the right position, look out! In short order, you *will* be successful.

Commit to following everything in this book for two years. In that time, you'll figure this game out and be on your way to success.

Two years may even sound too short. The wealthy write 10-year-plus plans. They invest the first couple of years in figuring things out. They improve and build a network and plan for the next three years. Finally, they maximize their opportunities in the last four or five years. By year ten, they can design a life with complete freedom to spend time on exactly what they choose instead of being forced (in return for money) to do what someone else tells them to do. Freedom is the ultimate goal.

Salespeople at any age can be incredibly impatient. Everyone wants the $100,000 sale and the commission that comes with it. You'll get there. The fundamentals work over time. As you follow the fundamentals, you're going to succeed.

The opposite is true as well. Start down the wrong path, and you'll find yourself selling bad products for a bad company making a bad salary. You'll be stuck, and at that point it becomes harder to get hired by a good company. The first two years are especially important to your future millionaire self. But you will not be a millionaire or have complete freedom of time during those first two years.

You need to ask yourself, *What do I have to do to be the most successful?* That's the question we'll answer together in these pages. Before you learn about closing more deals with more customers at higher rates, we have to cover the basics. Screw up the essentials, and you're just about messed up for life.

How you present yourself, how you get your act together, how you prove you're worth hiring and promoting in the first place . . . that's where we start. Because that's where every future millionaire salesperson's career starts.

# SO, YOU WANT TO MAKE IT IN SALES

Twelve years into my own sales journey, we had a company-wide sales meeting. All of our sales reps from around the world flew into our South Carolina HQ. We had acquired several companies by then, and I could see a big difference between the reps that had come through our hiring and training system and the ones that hadn't. The biggest difference was the alignment between what they liked to do and what they were doing. The natural job fit is key, and we will help you nail that for yourself.

People who ended up in sales by accident and had no training or career planning felt out of their depth. After a few drinks, they'd complain about how hard their jobs were. But the better the up-front job match was, the happier the salesperson, and the better the results.

Talk about a lightbulb moment. It's one I've had again and again as a sales trainer. If I get hired by a company to help their salespeople improve, I often learn that some of the salespeople are simply in the wrong job. It's because many salespeople are there by accident and have no career plan.

And frankly, half the people don't belong there. They aren't suited to be a salesperson. It would be like making me become an accountant or a mechanic overnight. I don't have those natural skills. I can turn a wrench if I have to, but I don't know enough about using tools to make a career out of being Mr. Fix-It. I'd set a car on fire just trying to fix the radio!

Now, how to read this book. Study it cover-to-cover. Do everything step-by-step because there is a method to the magic. It's like a recipe. You can't assemble the omelet before you've broken the eggs. So read one chapter, make sure you have it down pat, and move forward from there.

Take your time. Remember, you're playing the long game. You're a motivated person already, otherwise you wouldn't be taking the time to proactively learn how to optimize your selling, so don't expect cheesy motivation from me. I'm here to give you the cheat sheet on what works and what doesn't to get you rolling in sales.

If you're ready to learn everything I wish I'd known, let's get going.

# CHAPTER 2

# GET YOUR ACT TOGETHER. THIS IS NON-NEGOTIABLE.

N ed was a screwup. I was even worse for hiring him in the first place.

I made the rookie mistake of hiring too quickly to fill a spot. Ned seemed good enough. He was a nice guy with high energy and a good personality; he was gifted with the natural ability to ace first impressions.

Everything else about Ned was wrong. He talked too much on sales calls. He dressed like a slob. Most days he showed up late. He only met his quota once and had an excuse for everything. After another employee caught him smoking weed during lunch, I decided enough was enough. The next day I put it on my schedule to have a chat with Ned at 4:30 p.m. on the dot, but he showed up in my office around 11 a.m. that morning instead.

"Hey. I wonder if there's any way I could leave early today," he said.

"As a matter of fact, you can leave right now," I said. "We're done."

I have to take responsibility for hiring Ned. We never should have reached the point where he was even working for us. It was just as bad for Ned, because my mistake put him in the wrong job. I'm happy to report that he eventually figured things out and got his act together. He's successful today but in a different field.

The point is, you have to get your own act together before any- thing else in this book (or other sales books) is relevant. Gain control of your problem behaviors, and get out of your own way.

If you heard anything about sales before getting into the business, you probably expected to see high turnover. Over the last 10 years, the average sales rep's tenure with a company has fallen by half.[5] Salespeople usually blame their managers, their compensation, or the outright difficulty of sales. But if I was going to put money on it, I'd say the real reason has to do with the fact that most sales noobs just don't have their act together.

To be honest, neither did I when I started. And I didn't have this book to teach me how.

But I was lucky enough to have a great boss who pushed me forward. For every talented sales candidate I talk to (somebody with the right attitude and a willingness to learn), I've met nine Neds.

If guys like Ned had any self-awareness, they'd realize even *they* wouldn't hire themselves! Anyone who doesn't have their personal life under control won't do well on the job. That's especially true in sales.

Sales is the only job with a revenue quota, which makes it the most important job in any business. If your salespeople aren't selling, you don't have a business.

If Ned knew what it took to make it in sales, and if he got his act together, he might have survived year one. When you become aware of the things that can stop you from getting hired or promoted, you need to stop doing them immediately. If you learn what to do instead, you have a good shot at becoming a millionaire and achieving the successful, happy, free life you desire.

Quick tip: When you start doing well, don't allow your expenses to creep! Keep your cost of living as low as possible, even as you go

---

5    Matt Bertuzzi, "The 2018 SDR Metrics Report Is Here," Bridge Group, May 9, 2018, https://blog.bridgegroupinc.com/2018-sdr-metrics-report.

from earning $3,000 a month to $15,000 and higher. Even though my salespeople did very well for themselves, I wish I'd told them this fundamental of personal finance earlier because they'd be doing even better now and may have avoided making a few costly mistakes.

Right here at the start of your career is when you've got to get your act together. If you coast through the next few years on bad habits and laziness, you'll be mediocre at best. It'll be hard to recover. Not impossible, but it's an awful lot of extra work you don't need.

Let's get serious about the must-dos and must-don'ts right now.

## ACT LIKE A SALESPERSON

Success starts, and comes from, within. Present yourself well. That means a professional attitude and an appearance that makes you look like you belong. The specific style will vary depending on your industry, so take the time to look into what's expected. A good rule of thumb is to be yourself and keep in mind the sort of people you're selling to.

Being yourself means being your professional self, not your weekend self. If you have consistent problems with the police because of home altercations, it will reflect poorly on your work. I had a sales-person like that once, and I never really understood what was happening until after the fact. They had severe home issues, and those problems caused them to act odd at the office.

Don't do that. If you don't have your act together, it doesn't matter which job you find or how hard you work. If you're missing in action, you're not earning.

Other salespeople I've worked with have had alcohol and drug problems, gambling issues, and even love affairs with strippers. Since they kept their problems a secret, all I could see was the odd behavior. Anyone who couldn't get their problems under control eventually had to leave our sales organization. We were very willing to help if they owned up to their issues, but if we didn't know about their specific challenges, we had to base our decisions on their behavior and results.

All of the sales and motivational tricks in the world won't work until YOU are right and ready to roll. The good news is you don't have to be 100 percent perfect. Eighty percent and consistent behavior will place you far ahead of your competition.

# CHECK YOUR ATTITUDE

I met a young salesman named Thomas at a networking event. After we exchanged business cards, Thomas told me he'd been working for a good local company for two years, a competitor of mine at the time. Thomas was overweight and underdressed, with a dead look on his face. He whined about how his boss wasn't treating him right and how the business hadn't offered him a career path to the next promotion.

"I was thinking about going to grad school for my MBA. Do you think if I did that and graduated early, it might help me in the job market?" Thomas asked me.

"Would you like me to tell you the absolute truth, even if it's going to hurt your feelings?"

"Uh . . . sure, yeah."

"I wouldn't hire you under any condition, and neither would anybody else," I said. "No one wants to hear about your problems, no matter where you went to school or how good a guy you are."

"Um . . . OK."

"Get that blank stare off your face, stop talking, and start asking what you can do for your employer and your prospects. That's the only way you'll get your shit together."

Twelve months later, Thomas circled back with me.

"We haven't talked in a year," he said in a voicemail. "But I wanted to let you know our conversation changed my life. No one had ever told me that I was a whining, resting-bitch-faced loser complaining about life. Thank you for that."

I gave Thomas a call, one thing led to another, and I hired him. He's now a remarkable salesman and a good friend. If I hadn't urged

Thomas to get his act together, he may have stayed stuck on the "everything's bad" path where many salespeople stay their entire careers.

Think about how most alcoholics get treated. Nobody ever says to them, "Buddy, what's going on here?" when they've had one (or five) too many. People don't want to offend. So, they laugh it off—sometimes until someone's lying in a creek by the side of the road. I'm at a place in life where I don't care about hurting people's feelings. More importantly, I've realized that hurt feelings are often the only way to help people succeed. I can't live with myself if I don't say something to a person who needs the truth.

So, I'll say this to you as you're reading this right now . . . Get your act together. Be somebody you would hire.

## DON'T LOOK LIKE A SLOB

Appearance is as important as attitude. And I don't mean just how you dress. If a candidate walks in for an interview and their résumé is hard to read, has typos, or looks like it was formatted by a fifth-grader, they're gone. Why? If their résumé is screwed up, I guarantee the person behind it is, too.

If you don't dress well or you smell bad, nothing else matters. Am I saying you should wear a three-piece suit or a formal gown with pricey cologne or perfume? No. Simply maintain a pressed, clean, fresh look. Show you care about the details of your appearance—no wrinkles, broken zippers, or big stains. Not too flashy or attention-grabbing. Not too hot, not too cold—just right.

A young woman who worked for me a few years ago joined the sales team and was about to meet a customer for the first time, a customer who happened to own a company. When she asked me what she should wear, I told her whatever made her feel comfortable. Don't wear holey jeans, but don't dress up in a brand-new business suit. She showed up wearing what she normally wore to work, was herself in the meeting, and she did great. Our clients appreciated her and could tell she was at ease. If she'd worn some fancy, frilly business pantsuit she'd never worn before, she would have been fidgeting and on edge, and it would have shown. She was comfortable enough to be herself.

You can tell when someone tries to dress like they're part of a company, but it's out of their character. Don't pretend to be someone you're not. Dress like the professional version of you. Through behavior and appearance, you sell yourself, which builds trust and credibility, leading to sales success. My friend Ben is a classic Southern gentleman. He prefers blue jeans and a blazer to suits. Guess what? He gets hired wherever he interviews because he stands out. The managers who've hired Ben tell him they like that he dresses like himself for interviews. Other candidates wear leather or dry-cleaned suits and it's obvious they're not comfortable.

In other words, *professional* is open to interpretation. Before you pick out your "professional you" outfit, look at what kind of business you're heading into. That's why knowing your best-fit company is so important, which we'll get into in Chapter 3. For now, just know that you may need to shift your appearance a *little* so you're dressing the part. When I've worked at start-ups and early-stage companies, we wanted hires who looked like us. We wanted the tech-whiz kids in flip-flops and shorts who didn't have any idea what they couldn't do. If someone came in wearing a suit, it made us nervous!

Sound confusing? Being comfortable yet professional, as with everything in life, isn't black and white. Simply be mindful of how your attitude and appearance make important people perceive you, and you're already further ahead than most salespeople gunning for the same customers you are. Don't waste this incredible advantage.

If you're a dude, one last thing: Unless your boss wears an earring, you don't wear an earring. Same goes for tattoos, piercings, and other body mods that people can see. They won't help—and will likely hurt—your chances of getting the future you want, even if nobody tells you about it.

| The Attributes of Successful Salespeople: How Many Do You Have? | | |
|---|---|---|
| | Yes | No |
| Are you clean? | | |
| Can you speak coherently? | | |
| Do you dress professionally? | | |
| Do you have a college degree? | | |
| Do you have a recommendation from someone who works at your first company? | | |
| Does your Kolbe sales score match the position you are interviewing for? | | |
| Do you live in the area where you would be working? | | |
| Are you an extrovert? | | |
| You don't have a face tattoo or a pornstache? (Everyone should get one point here for showing up without a pornstache!) | | |
| Have you ever received a sales commission? | | |
| 1. Write your number of "Yes" answers here: ___ / 10. <br> 2. Convert the fraction into a percentage (e.g., 4 / 10 becomes a 40 percent chance to succeed). <br> **How likely are you to succeed in sales?_____ %** | | |

This chart is a good jumping-off point to assess your appeal. Your unique attributes are assets that can help you find the right spot as a new salesperson. The most important things to do here are 1) work on your personal skill set continually, 2) find the companies that best fit you, and 3) be comfortable being yourself along the way.

What aspects of your score can you control? You can improve most of them with just a little knowledge, and with the world of internet learning at our fingertips, you have no excuse but to ace the attribute test. If you are worried about other external factors like your age or gender or religion or sexual preference, then you need to understand something. The world (and specifically the world of commerce) takes all that into consideration when making hiring decisions. If hiring to a cer- tain profile has proven to be better for the revenue of a certain company, then they will give that some weight.

Keep in mind that this can work both for you and against you. As you create your list of ideal places to work, don't let previous hiring patterns that work against you stop you from going for the job. In the same vein, if you find great companies that seem more likely to give you a chance based on your profile, I would start with them.

You probably won't read this anywhere else, but you deserve to know the truth.

## DON'T FORGET YOUR PERSONAL PRIORITIES

Salespeople who don't cut it are often, surprisingly, the ones who start off hot and seem to have a bright future. If you watched them in action, you'd wish for their ability to think on their feet and speak with persuasion. Many have been blessed with loads of natural sales talent, but because it comes so easy, they take their eyes off the ball and make mistakes.

What goes wrong? They mess up their life priorities—their health, relationships, or personal finances (or all three)—and get mired in bad decisions. These three essentials must be in place and under control if you're going to pursue a meaningful career in sales or anywhere else. Here's how to keep them straight.

## TAKE CARE OF YOURSELF

Make health and wellness part of your day, every day. This is a simple cheat code for success. Get in good shape and exercise for an hour a day. Lift weights, do yoga, or walk or run outside. Do whatever you like to do sports-wise, as long as it's something that gets you going for at least an hour every day.

It is going to be a lot easier for you to succeed if you take care of yourself. The exercise will help with your physical and mental health, and also your sales numbers. Trust me on this one. Mental and physical fitness enables you to do your best work. There are already plenty of books on this subject, but here's my short version:

- Exercise an hour a day (any type as long as you do it daily).
- Drink two big glasses of water as soon as you wake up. Just gulp it down. And then, as the day goes on, try to add eight more glasses. Morning saturation is a great hack because your body needs it most then, and it gets you started on your water goal for the day.
- Sleep at least seven hours every night. Among other things, sleeping is like rebooting your body's computer—everything has a chance to rest and reset for the next cycle. The longer you go without a good reset the more likely you will feel tired, sluggish, or grumpy, and have a bad attitude. You want to get your body into a rhythm of wake-up time and bedtime. An "Opportunity Alarm" on your phone is a good start for the morning, and you can do the same with a bedtime reminder. It sounds weird if you haven't done it, but it works. You will feel better and function better when you get into a rhythm.

These three basics are a great start. Like I said, you can get advanced information on nutrition and all types of tactics and methods for functioning at the highest levels. That information is available for free on the Internet. I am all for it and am constantly looking for new tweaks to help me work and live better. But, like anything else, I recommend you start with some basics, get them into your life, and build from there.

Daily exercise, 10 glasses of water, and a regular sleep pattern. Make sure you have these down pat, and keep adding from there.

Notice I'm not encouraging triathlon training or six-pack abs or bodybuilding. I'm also not telling you to forsake all your free time to live at work and close, close, close. People who overdo anything have to cut corners in other areas of their lives. The salespeople I've known who go ballistic at marathons, weightlifting, or other extreme exercises flame out at work. They can barely walk into the office the morning after CrossFit. And spending more time talking about what they do for exercise rather than discussing the problems they're solving for customers is not a good sign. Sales jobs are difficult enough without putting your body through trauma for the sake of fitness. You need to be able to focus when you sit down at your desk.

Work out an hour a day, drink water, sleep.

People whose sales managers demand high performance "at any cost" leave their employees equally imbalanced. These salespeople end up eating doughnuts for breakfast, chugging coffee all day, and smoking and drinking away their evenings and weekends. Welcome to burnout. Both extremes—too much fitness or not enough—are shortsighted.

Successful, healthy salespeople have sustainable routines. They get in decent shape and stay there. I advise you to do the same as soon as possible.

When I was in my twenties, I thought it was a badge of honor to have no work-life balance. I thought I couldn't be successful unless I worked evenings and weekends and took no time to take care of myself. I thought personal vacation days were bullshit. I didn't even exercise every day. Seems pretty stupid now.

## BOOZE BONUS

This is a tricky one, as most young folks drink. I sure did.

Of the first 100 salespeople I hired, here's a brutally honest break- down (from memory):

- 12 did not drink at all.
- 75 enjoyed regular drinking and kept it under control.
- 4 enjoyed drinking and occasionally did something because of the booze that caused huge problems for themselves and others.
- 9 graduated from enjoying drinking to becoming full-blown alcoholics.

Of those last nine, not one of them started out as an alcoholic. They weren't even problem drinkers. They gradually increased the count until they had a problem that got out of control. Several were able to stop and be happy again without alcohol, but many did not end well at all.

I say this so you see what can happen. Please be aware that having an alcohol challenge is not something that people do on purpose. Some folks, usually around 10 percent, have a progressive reaction that causes them big problems. Others are fine.

From a business perspective, if a business owner or manager has a chance to hire or promote a big-time party boozer or someone who either doesn't drink or has no issue, what do you think they are going to do? What would you do?

Be realistic about your alcohol consumption. Take proactive steps to keep it under control. Specifically, if you are not sure, book an hour with a therapist that helps with alcohol/substance addictions, etc. It doesn't hurt to have a private conversation with a pro (I am sure of it).

## Win Mentors and Influence People (and Don't Marry a Stripper)

They say you become the average of the five people you hang around most. I can tell you for certain that quality relationships ultimately show up in higher commissions. If you're hanging around a bunch of ne'er-do-wells who aren't going anywhere, you'll become a miscreant, too.

Especially stay away from the complainers and whiners. Find the winners and hang around them instead.

My friend Brad barely got through the University of Michigan. When Brad wasn't waiting tables, he drank gallons of beer and hit the bong as often as possible. He somehow made it through school, and after college, he kept the restaurant job and the bad habits. Soon Brad was 26 years old with no plan and way behind his peers.

When an old college pal came into town, he took Brad out for dinner at a classy steak house. Brad's buddy worked for IBM, had a company car and an expense account, and was on a strong arc to continued success and a happy life. That night was Brad's wake-up call to take life seriously, associate with better people, and get a better job. Brad went back to get his MBA, restarted his life, and eventually started a great global business. He had to work very hard to make up for lost ground.

It's certainly possible to come back from mistakes, but remember how much easier it would have been for him (and will be for you) to get started on a good path from the jump.

There's something magical about associating with quality people. In a world of 7.5 billion, find your five or ten. The number doesn't matter; the quality does.

When I was in my twenties, I met with seven other technology sales professionals once a week for breakfast. We all were in our twenties, lived in the same city, and had a strong interest in technology and sales. Today, every one of those seven has built and run the biggest technology companies in the Southeastern US. Some have done it a few times, and one of the seven has built a company that does over $4 billion a year! All stay in touch and continue to help each other as we go forward.

You can build this in your life on purpose. Find the winners in your chosen focus area and set something up on a regular basis to talk shop and help each other. Consciously spend time with people who could be important to your career someday. This goes beyond watercooler hangouts and industry networking. Strategic relationships add value to everyone. Put yourself in the company of people going in the same direction as you are.

Start with the people at your current company. Figure out who the real winners are. Not the coolest or most popular, but the most respected and hardest working. Get to know them. They have the inside scoop on everything in the business and the industry that you won't get any-where else. Enlist them as your mentors. How? Just ask!

Many people don't do this because they're intimidated. The fact is, many professionals *want* to offer guidance to others simply because it feels good knowing someone wants to learn from them. Also, commit to this positive networking on a regular basis. You will get your best benefits down the line, not at the first meeting.

Outside of work, you can appoint yourself the leader by sending out once-a-week-for-breakfast email invitations. Ask prospects, influencers within the community, people you want to be friends with—whoever you want to join you. Start small. Treat these uplifting relationships like royalty. Show interest, share experiences, learn from them, and maybe make a sale. While you're at it, be aware of people who personify the worst in sales—Negative Nellies and pity-partiers who only talk about how bad things are. Avoid these folks at all costs! Don't try to change them, just back away.

My counsel applies to your personal life as well. Do *not* get stuck with crazy. It's almost eerie how often my salespeople who married young are bothered by their spouses at work. If you're trying to focus on building a career, getting stuck with a neurotic partner for life lowers the odds of success more than just about anything. If I were your life coach, I would tell you—man or woman—to stay single until you are at least 25 years old *and* earning $100,000 a year. Get your- self together before you buy a house or bring another person into your world. Then you can afford the big wedding, destination honeymoon, and two and a half kids (and pets).

I've had numerous young sales guys come into my office, close the door, and ask my advice about their girlfriend or fiancée. "If you're asking my opinion," I always tell them, "she's still going to be here in a year. Why don't you hit your numbers and get your apartment, car, and student loans paid off before taking things to the next level? Tell her your goals and she'll understand."

In one of these impromptu romance advice conversations, one sales-man admitted that Shadow, his bride-to-be, was a stripper.

"Historically, most stripper marriages have bad odds," I told him bluntly. "If I were you, I'd run as fast as I could to get away from her. But promise me you won't tell her I said anything. Whatever you decide, I want no part in your relationship with Shadow."

When I said that, I had no reason to think she was insane. But I had a hunch. The next day, my employee left town with Shadow and got married at a courthouse in the next county.

Three days later, she pulled a gun on him.

She shot out a window in their new apartment, then called the police on *him*. She fled before they arrived. We set up remote work arrangements for my employee a few days later in a different state because I was afraid Shadow would do a drive-by at our office, where she knew he worked. Last anyone heard of Shadow, she had disappeared. Whew. Needless to say, that episode made building his sales career very difficult.

A stable personal life provides the certainty every successful salesperson needs. Unstable relationships do the opposite. Commission selling is a high-risk, high-reward business. If you're going to make it, you need all the support you can get. This isn't a marriage book, but at the same time, your personal life influences whether you become a sales superstar. If you get married at 16 and have 14 kids, that doesn't mean you can't whoop some ass. It'll just be harder. If your spouse and family support you, that helps a lot.

Think about which friendships and relationships will boost your success and which will detract from it. Only you can decide who you want in your camp. If you can only have 10 absolute best friends, make sure you choose them versus them choosing you. Be intentional about your relationships.

## GET YOUR MONEY TOGETHER

There are no perfect financial goals to set, no flawless budgets to follow, and no risk-free investments to make. Too many variables, such as your age, job, location, and preferences, make one-size-fits-all advice useless.

That said, what I'm about to share with you is based on the experience of more than 100 highly successful and happy salespeople, which includes a few dozen millionaires. What did they do with their money? More importantly, what did they *not* do? What do they wish they'd done instead? Everything I teach about building a financial foundation is based on their (and my) reflections.

Whatever you do, keep your living expenses as low as possible. Many sales jobs pay you an hourly wage or a small salary with a commission on top of that. Use your base pay to cover basics like rent, food, and toilet paper. Put whatever is left toward an emergency fund so you're not out of luck if another coronavirus comes along. Stable income with few expenses is easier said than done, I know. But it can be accomplished.

If you want to be able to replace your job with passive income, enjoy zero financial pressure for the rest of your life, and work on what you want when and where you want to, start saving. Save all the commissions you earn above your base compensation and put them toward long-term assets.

An asset is an investment that makes money while you sleep. Buy a bunch of assets, and life becomes one big, delightful playground. What kind of assets could you save up for? Some salespeople I know read real estate books during lunch breaks. They buy one new property a year. Others study the stock market and buy shares of companies that pay regular dividends. If you're not handy with property and know next to nothing about stocks, then an annuity may be a better fit. If your employer offers you 401(k) matching, you may want to accept it (this is where the company matches some or all the money you invest every month via an automatic paycheck deduction).

All you need is an asset (or assets) that safely provides the monthly income you want. Planning your financial future is simple math. If you want to earn $10,000 a month in passive income, save up those commissions until you've hit $2 million. Then you might consider an annuity that pays investors 0.5 percent of the principal every month. It's possible to save big numbers like these even if you sell cheap cell phones rather than enterprise software. Several multimillionaire salespeople I work with "made it" in their 40s or 50s. They weren't cashing five- or six-figure commission checks at 28 years old because they sold low-ticket services and consumer products. Even if you *never* walk away from an enterprise sale with a seven-figure commission like John Harrison or Crystal Novella, you'll still end up in the top 10 percent over time. And that's the *worst-case* scenario.

---

That said, earning money is one skill. Keeping and growing it is another. I know successful entrepreneurs who make a lot of money, but they're always broke by the end of the month. Resist the temptation to spend your money right away. Sure, you *want* that new electric car, that big-screen TV, that penthouse apartment, that trip to Amsterdam. But if dropping thousands of dollars now means you'll have to put off financial freedom for another 10 or 20 years, is it worth it?

Whatever your income looks like, choose the steady path to success. It's the only one that can take you to a reality where you never have to work another day in your life. No matter how much you want a Rolex or a mansion, delay your gratification. One day, you'll be grateful you did—because you'll be a millionaire.

Try to go fast and you probably won't get what you want long-term. Go slow and steady with regular monthly contributions, and you will get the financial future you desire.

Does putting off treating yourself to expensive possessions and experiences mean no hobbies? No. Don't live an empty life you hate. But certain hobbies can be a distraction from your time and your savings. Maybe you want to travel or play golf. Ask yourself: *Should I spend time and money on this or use those resources to set myself up for financial freedom?* That's a leading question if there ever was one. Because you already know the right answer. Getting your act together means doing the right thing at the right time. When you handle your monthly expenses and your monthly savings contribution first, you can go on that golf trip guilt-free.

# OBEY THE 80 PERCENT RULE

With your health, relationships, and finances, aim to be consistent not perfect. Perfection is an idiot's pursuit and usually leads to a boom/ bust cycle. A balanced life is better than perfectionism because the ideal world doesn't exist.

Think disciplined consistency, not absolute perfection. Put a process in place to support your targets in life and work the process every day.

Consistency isn't an all-or-nothing endeavor. If you're fifteen minutes late for work one day, forget your tie, or skip exercise to stay up late Friday night, don't beat yourself up. As long as you stay about 80 percent consistent, you're good. In keeping with the famous 80/20 rule, doing the right thing 80 percent of the time puts you in the top 20 performers. Nobody ever hits the mark 100 percent.

Aim for 80 percent, and you will earn a reputation as a stable, reliable, trustworthy salesperson. You'll move steadily up the food chain. And you'll be ready when your occasional breakthroughs come.

## DON'T WAIT TO BE TOLD WHAT TO DO

How do you get ahead in sales to earn the big commissions? Do what you're supposed to do. You'd be surprised how few salespeople do this.

Unclear expectations are often the culprit. But it's your job as the employee to figure out what you should be accomplishing. The very lowest bar is the expectation of your company—the minimum you must do to not get fired. What's expected of you? Thirty-two prospect interactions a day by email, phone, or whatever method is available? Three face-to-face meetings per day? Fifty touches in the customer relationship management (CRM) system?

To move past noob status, figure out what expectations your employer has of you. Put in the effort to be in the top 20 percent year after year, and you will win at this game.

## USE CHECKLISTS (BUT DON'T BE AN IDIOT)

Create a checklist of actions you follow every day.

Sales leaders often write their sequence of specific activities, such as an expected number of calls and completing a new sales training module. Only idiot salespeople start at 8:00 a.m. with their only goal being "make sales today and leave by five." Successful sellers plan to win before the day begins.

For example, first thing in the morning, many recite a personal mantra or affirmation. "I am unstoppable—I have a process in place that will help me achieve everything in life I set out to do. I am a top performer in everything I do." What could yours be? Take whatever negative self-talk you've got running through your head and replace it with its opposite, positive message. You could even write it down and post it on your bathroom mirror or put it as a repeat calendar item so you see it when you boot up every day.

We're all faced with negative inputs in our minds every day. It could be bad news, negative people, or bad self-talk. Take control first thing in the morning to put some positive messages into your brain. Start the day filling up your brain on purpose with your best messaging.

If possible, complete the most important (and the hardest) tasks before noon. Prep your call list and put it on your checklist. Print your sales call and follow-up list on one page so you can see it at a glance. Make the calls as soon as you get to work.

As much as possible, keep reactive tasks off your to-do list, such as getting sucked into non-essential emails or doing data entry. Once you've completed the tasks that lead toward the sale, then you can spend time reacting. If you tackle work as it comes at you or randomly do whatever throughout the day, you'll be an idiot with no momentum.

Everyone needs structure. Sure, there are exceptions to the rule, but I've learned that disciplined and consistent preparation is the most likely route to success.

Simple rule starting out: Start your day with some healthy self-talk, get your prospecting done, complete all of your other calls, get your exercise, and do a little continuous improvement training. It's incredibly important to get your prospecting done first, otherwise (I know this from experience) it won't happen.

Following that flow creates a pretty good day. You'll get a little bit better every day and nail your goals. But give it time to work. There are no shortcuts.

Not all noobs have a flexible schedule. In that case, tackle some activities before and after work. It's easy to make excuses about why we can't do things and don't have time. But the company doesn't have control over your whole life. I'm not saying you should be working on your to-do list until 9:00 p.m. It's important and appropriate to create boundaries that support balance.

Before or after work, spend half an hour resetting your brain by doing something creative. I'm a jazz musician, so I play music. Some people garden, write poetry, or paint. Whatever gives you a creative outlet to refresh mentally. To make sure you have time for this, set an alarm every night. Happy, successful people get up early—between 5:00 and 6:00 a.m. One of the first things you should do when your feet hit the floor is write and review that daily checklist, like a pilot making their checks before a flight.

## DON'T BE LATE WITH A BISCUIT

In 20 years, I've never known a salesperson who was habitually late and went on to a great career. They're either mediocre salespeople, or they washed up years ago and left the business. If you can manage to start work 30 minutes early 80 percent of the time, you show the boss you can be trusted to lead. It's almost a sure thing that the first person in wins the sales contest over time.

I'm not here to tell you that you should spend twelve hours at the office every day. All I'm saying is that if you want to be a successful noob, you're not going to be the last to show up or the first to leave. People who crawl in late and sneak out early have a zero percent chance of success. The boss may not see them, but the slacking shows up on reports. They can hang around for a while but are headed down a bad path and maybe don't even know it yet.

Act like a winner, follow the process laid out here like a winner, and you will be a winner—just allow some time for proof.

## DON'T GET CONTROVERSIAL

If you want to succeed in any job, stay quiet about how screwed up politicians are. You need to focus on achieving your goals, not spouting off with your opinion.

These are huge distractions that will piss off half your colleagues, prospects, and customers. This includes in-person and online. Before the Internet, there was only one way to blow a chance—by screwing up the interview. The Internet gives noobs dozens of ways to disqualify themselves.

When I'm vetting sales candidates, I look them up on social media. If I find something negative or hateful about religion, politics, or sexual orientation, that's a hard pass. What I do is standard procedure with folks that hire in sales, and they won't tell you about it. You just don't get the job.

Business owners in a town or a specific industry often know each other and share information about candidates. Sometimes they will refer a candidate to their friend that just doesn't fit right. They send up red flags on social media or have a bad reputation. When I see that, I'll warn other business owners I know never to hire them. If the person had an interview scheduled with me, I'll cancel and say, "It just didn't work out."

And if you piss off a crazy internet group, they might bombard your Google or Yelp listing with fake one-star reviews.

Word travels fast; you can't afford a negative reputation in busi- ness. If you want to be a good noob, keep your convictions to yourself.

## DON'T SAVE THE WORLD

I think it's great to volunteer and support nonprofits. But whatever your charitable act of choice is, if you're a sales noob, stay focused on the main job at hand.

Do-gooding on the job is annoying. You were hired to help the owner of the company focus on the objectives of the business. Why would they want to pay you to distract others from those objectives? Owners often don't come out and say it because they want to keep the peace, but they will treat you differently and not in a way you want. You'll miss out on promotions, raises, and other growth opportunities. When there are layoffs, you'll be the first to go. You may not even get hired in the first place if in an interview you go on and on about the nonprofit where you volunteer.

In short, if you do try to save the world, stay quiet about it, don't distract others at work, and keep it to yourself. Make your numbers first. Earn the right to take time off to do good.

You're giving some things up now to become the best salesperson you can be. As you save your commissions and build up assets, you can afford to do whatever you want with your money and time.

## DON'T THINK YOU KNOW EVERYTHING

Most young people just starting out (including me when I started) think they know how things should be done.

Take my advice and keep your mouth shut at the beginning.

Watch and learn. Get six months at least under your belt. Learn your company's selling process, master it, get a bunch of reps and practice in, and earn a spot at the table. The time may come when your boss asks, "What do you think we could do better?" Be ready. Even better, have some anecdotal data to support your findings. The likely destination from following this path is VP of sales or owner. Both will be places to share your ideas and make decisions. For now, take your time.

Bottom line, don't do stupid things. Respect your boss and your coworkers. Do what you're supposed to do at least 80 percent of the time, and you will steadily improve. You'll set and achieve bigger quotas for a long, successful sales career and have plenty of great options as you progress.

Remember, you can't go back and do your first year over again. The year-one company you work with and the habits you establish are the basis for your future.

Weird but true fact: Your year one will be much lower paid than your year 10, but will be 5x more important to your future. What happens in year 10 is an outcome of how you started.

# DON'T ASSUME THE MILLIONS START IN YEAR ONE

The habits of millionaire salespeople begin long before the millions roll in. Habits like getting to work on time, taking the time to person- ally understand what the customer's going through (getting your hands dirty), and learning what problem you are solving for the customer are all essential components.

Do what you're supposed to do—and avoid what you aren't— beginning in year one, and you're practically guaranteed to be a million-dollar sales/businessperson one day. Maybe by year five and certainly by year ten.

But only if you do what you're supposed to do and skip the bullshit. When you say you're going to talk to 20 people a day, make the calls you're supposed to make. The millions don't start in year one, but the process does. As always, remember that the process only starts roll- ing once you choose to take sales seriously.

And be mindful and careful as you make planning decisions about your business beginning.

You can be a clown in year one, or have an average crappy year, and still blame it on being a rookie. And you can do the right things with discipline and only have an OK year because you're still learning.

You'll probably have a new territory. You're not going to have rapport with customers yet. You're going to have low-momentum opportunities. It takes time, persistence, and understanding to reach the close.

Don't let the numbers fool you. If you're doing the right thing, you will get there eventually, and only a lack of patience or discipline can slow you down. That said, you may not feel like a perfect fit right away. That's OK. The beginning is when you should focus on doing exactly what the company playbook recommends. One of my sales trainers called this phase getting "dirty reps," where you know the sales call is not perfect but you are doing it anyway to get the reps in and to practice and improve.

When you start out, neither your manager nor other salespeople expect immediate results. No one who is successful or positive to work for will, at least. But it's normal to put pressure on ourselves, so remember at the beginning to focus on the process and not the outcome. Trust that the rewards will come in time. I've encountered countless sales organizations, and if a sales rep is following the process and has a great positive attitude, I have never seen a company cut bait early. Relax and stay with the process.

For some, that wait is longer than three months, while for others it's less. If you give me a smart college grad, in 30 days I'll teach them the product and the script, and we'll do a whole bunch of practice calls. By month two, they'll have a territory and they're going to recite the script in their sleep. They're also finding opportunities, and we're work- ing together to convert them to sales.

As a noob, if you find the opportunities, your manager should be able to help close them. Every company is going to be different based on the complexity of what they sell. Typically, the higher the ticket, the more prep and training it requires to get in the game.

Having said that, your secret mindset from the outset needs to be, *how can I generate a lot of revenue for this company on day one? What can I think of that will make it happen? If there's anything holding me back, how can I overcome that?*

If you have a good fit to begin with and you follow the correct process, you can make your sales on-ramp more like a runway. You'll fly while others are still puttering along. That doesn't mean you should kill yourself trying to win deals. Some people say, "I'm going to make a thousand calls a day," or "I'm going to sleep in the office." That doesn't work in the long run.

Just be solid. Do your job. If you follow a good process and aim for 80 percent, with time you're going to be successful. And never forget the bigger play for the company. Often the largest mega deals are not in the normal pipeline and may be discouraged by management. They will say it's a distraction and "too big to happen," etc. The reps with vision keep nudging these along until they are ready for primetime.

I saw a tweet once that stuck with me. It said the quick and dirty get-rich-and-successful plan is this: Pick your area of expertise and spend five years getting great at it, get yourself into ownership in that area with your own entity or with partners, and build that business for five years or so, until you have the model figured out where you can grow steadily and make money. At that point, you can run it until you want to cash out. Usually by this time, running the business is fun; the value increases every year, so staying can be a great choice. The longer you stay, the more you can sell it for one day when you want out.

We get tricked a little when we read about Silicon Valley-type start-ups where you can go from ideas to millions in just a few years. Most of these stories leave out how many years those winners trained and worked to be in a position to make some of these projects happen. Think 20 years. From age 20-25, learn the biz; from 25-30, find a way to ownership; from 30-40, build the biz and your equity. At 40, you have choices!

# DON'T NOOB YOURSELF

Salespeople noob themselves in their everyday routine. We covered the worst ways in the previous sections about getting your act together. There are also beginner mistakes that slow down the process, such as poorly handled objections, failure to negotiate, or facts-based sales pitches that fall flat.

Other ways salespeople screw up:

- Calling prospects too much and trying to talk them into something.
- Not giving the prospect a chance to talk.
- Winging every sales call.
- Letting negative self-talk stop you.
- Expecting unrealistic results.

This book is not merely a collection of sales wisdom gathered over my 30-year career. Here and elsewhere, I'm focusing on your first couple of years to prevent you from noobing yourself—doing all the wrong things because you didn't know better. We'll get into prospecting, sales calling, and negotiating soon.

This is where head trash comes in. Noobing yourself is not just what you do and don't do, it's also what you think. When you believe something wrong about sales, about the prospect, or about yourself that doesn't do you any favors, that's head trash. These might be common misconceptions or personal shortcomings you think you have. In the chapters ahead, we'll rummage through head trash on each topic (e.g., prospecting) and take it out to the dump for good.

Not everyone has the same head trash, but everyone has some. For example, a lot of kids right out of college think trash like this:

- *I'm settling for sales because I couldn't get a better job.*
- *Every time I make a call, I feel like I'm interrupting.*
- *I don't look approachable enough.*
- *I suck.*

During my early years, I assumed that if I wasn't selling as much as the ten-year pros, I was a failure. I was so wrong. Noobs must judge themselves based on process in the first couple of years, not results. Sure, you want to be a great salesperson right out of the shoot, but you've got process work to do.

For the time being, your priority is to follow the path I'm laying out for you.

# CHAPTER 3

# KNOW WHAT YOU'RE ABOUT

**D**o you want to get good at something you hate doing? I didn't think so. Nobody does.

This is a major reason why so many sales noobs wash up and burn out. They take the first sales job they can get, or maybe the one that pays the most or sounds the coolest, and it's often not the right one for them. Then they're stuck selling things they don't care about to a group of clients they don't match up with. It's a downward spiral.

If you're spinning round and round in one now, what can you do?

If you're looking for a sales job, how do you avoid this mess and find the right fit?

You need to know what you're about.

That's why I recommend that you don't take the first sales job that comes along. You're launching yourself down a path that can change later, but it's painful to change because you're investing time in relationships and networking and knowledge. Don't jump into a job you hate that will set you back. If you know what you want, and you are patient and confident, you can find the right fit.

That's not to say being in a less than ideal job is the end of the world. Just don't stay there. And even if you haven't found your perfect job right away, you can still be doing all the positive sales things. You come in early, you're good on the phone, you make the calls, you follow the script, yet you're looking for other opportunities. When you are not in the ideal situation—while you wait—love the one you're with, and do all the right things so when you get to your perfect spot, you'll be ready to roll!

## TEST YOURSELF BEFORE YOU WRECK YOURSELF

People are naturally happier and more productive when they're free to be themselves. When they're aware of the key personality traits that make them tick—and really understand the core of who they are—that's when they can do their best work.

Remember sales expert Bill Lee? After growing a start-up to $640 million in sales, he and his team sold the company and he started Lee Resources, a sales consulting firm with a twist. In addition to offering his sales expertise, Bill emphasized candidate profiling and psychological testing for hiring. When I started having doubts about my hiring strategy, I decided it was time to get his opinion. Knowing his reputation and track record of success as a business and sales leader in Greenville, I knew I could trust Bill's insights and knowledge.

"What hiring profile are you using to identify your top sales candidates?" Bill asked during our initial meeting.

"We don't have a specific profile," I said. "If I personally like a candidate or if the person comes highly recommended, they're hired. Unfortunately, I've noticed this method isn't working in our favor. Our team consists of vastly different skill sets, personalities, educa- tional backgrounds, and temperaments, which has led to inconsistent performance."

Side note—This is a great example of head trash. I thought I knew what I was doing, so I kept doing it until Bill taught me otherwise.

"I'd like to suggest that you try something," said Bill. "What if we ask your top sales performers to take a profile test? We could compare their results, identify any traits these employees share, and then hire future applicants who also have those characteristics."

I'm always willing to give a new idea a chance, so I agreed. We asked 10 of our top salespeople to take Bill's profile test and used the resulting data to create a profile of our ideal candidate. Armed with this information, we incorporated Bill's profiling system into our hiring process and used it to focus on certain traits when making our next round of hires.

Through testing, we were able to better understand our employees. We saw what their natural talents were and how they instinctively took (or avoided taking) action in different situations. The method proved successful; it allowed us to narrow the field and hire only those who matched the qualities identified in our hiring profile, ultimately leading to increased sales.

This strategy taught me a valuable lesson. When people are aware of their key strengths and weaknesses, they're more successful. And this is true whether they're at work or pursuing a hobby.

Since that first meeting with Bill, our profile testing process has evolved. The profiling technology I use in my businesses today is called the Kolbe A index. This test differs from others you may have heard of. It doesn't measure IQ or categorize personality traits. Instead, it measures a person's instincts about why and how they do things. And it identifies natural strengths and weaknesses.

Another reason I like this testing platform is that it's available to anyone. You can take the test online for around $50. You can find the link through my website at www.SchoolForNoobs.com. Of everything in this book, getting your Kolbe done—and understanding it—is a top-five recommendation. A true game-changer.

I know what you're thinking. When you're just starting your career, 50 bucks might seem like a lot of money. But let's set that price tag aside for a moment. Remember what I said about people being happier when they get to be themselves? That means they're also happier when they have a job that fits their personality. When you actively use the self-knowledge you get from profile testing, the benefits of that level of awareness last a lifetime. Doesn't that make your career—and you—worthy of a little investment? In my experience, discovering your innate talents and learning how to leverage them to succeed makes good business sense and will save you a lot of time spent working against your tendencies.

What sort of things will the Kolbe A tell you about yourself? While working on a school project or a task at work, have you ever noticed:

- if there's a time of day when you feel most productive?
- if you work best independently in absolute silence or if you thrive when collaborating in a boisterous group?
- how you react when someone gives you a task. Are you eager to get started, or do you need time to formulate a plan?
- in times of stress, do you withdraw from others or throw yourself into activity?

Taking a profile test like the Kolbe A will give you a competitive edge that helps you perform at your best, even in your first year on the job. You'll also be able to tell whether your current employer (or a potential future employer) is the right fit for you.

Stop right here and take it now. I'll wait: kolbe.com/kolbe-a-index/

. . .

You took the Kolbe A! Welcome back. Now that you know what you're about, you can make an informed decision to sell products or services you care about for a company you actually like. If that's not the story at your current job, make a change.

Now, instead of plunging into a wide search for a new job that could be just as bad as your current one, you'll be able to look for a position that aligns with your strengths and brings you some happiness. Just wait until you find that new role before giving your two weeks' notice.

When you put the work in, no matter what your current position is, you never know when the right opportunity is just around the corner. As I recounted earlier, I had this happen when I went to Best Buy. When I walked in, the salesperson said, "Hey, big guy. What'd you come in for today?" I told him I was looking for a TV.

Normally you never give that information to salespeople. It's like your secret. When someone says, "Can I help you?" we say we're "just looking." He helped me by asking why I was looking for a TV. I explained it to him. He took me right where I wanted to go. He knew my budget and said, "This one's $200 more, but it's Japanese. If it was me, I'd go with the Japanese."

He did a great job; he got me exactly what I needed without taking too much of my time. Perfect. It was probably because he'd been in a successful sales position in Chicago for many years and was semi-retired. He took this job to have something to do. It was the first time I had encountered a professional in a retail environment.

What he did is duplicable. It's not that hard. It's all about asking a different question and trying to determine what the person wants, and then helping them get it. Because he was so good, I hired him. That same story could be anybody today who's doing a great job, even if they don't like their current position.

Great companies will find great people wherever they are, so don't wait for the perfect fit to do your best work.

This is not a guarantee, but it's common for someone who's doing a notably good job in a retail sales environment to get hired by the customers who shop there. You can be like the Best Buy guy and go from making $15,000 to $20,000 per year to making $40,000 to $50,000 per year—that was the minimum he was going to make with me. He did much better than that as an inside salesperson. He more than doubled his income, and it happened in a moment.

As an employer, I made a split-second decision. I saw that this guy was good and wanted him on our team. He was smart. He knew what he was doing.

He worked for us for several years, but he was semi-retired and didn't want to work full time. If things were like they are now with all this flex time, I would have kept him forever and said, "Work three hours a week. We'll figure it out." And that whole working relationship spawned from his retail job.

If you work retail and you haven't been approached yet to put your résumé in for higher-paying jobs, there's a reason. You're the reason.

If you had your act together, had a big smile on your face, were excited about life, and looked presentable, someone would have approached you already.

This "get hired up" phenomenon also happens all the time when one employee leaves a company for a promotion and "brings" a few key people with them. It could be a vendor hiring a salesperson to come work for them. It happens all the time.

The key takeaway here is that when you're at work, you're getting noticed by everyone around you. And it's not only your manager that can give you a promotion!

# SELL THE RIGHT STUFF FOR THE RIGHT COMPANY IN THE RIGHT PLACE

Picking your first sales job is more important than choosing which college to attend. While you let that sink in, let me tell you about Bubba Britton.

Bubba was the Clemson University Tiger mascot. I hired him out of college to work at our software start-up. He was a super high-energy personality, and his colleagues loved him, but he only had average sales numbers. I was always scratching my head, wondering why Bubba's sales didn't match his extroversion and how much I liked him. So, I sat down with him and had "the talk."

"There's no one I'd rather go out for a beer with," I said to Bubba. "I hope to do that with you for the rest of my life. But if you don't hit your numbers this month, I'm going to have to fire you."

Bubba put his shoulder to the grindstone and improved his numbers. But then I learned why he wasn't doing better. Bubba didn't love what we were selling, nor did he enjoy inside sales, which involved sitting in front of a computer in an office all day. It was a bad fit.

Eventually, he found his way back to Clemson, where he's now one of the key fundraisers in the Clemson alumni network. He goes to various Clemson booster clubs (in person) and rubs elbows with other people who love the Tigers. There's no one in the country better at that job because he's so well suited for it. He gets to be a cheerleader for the school minus the hot mascot suit.

When he was working for me, he didn't love it. We sold complicated software to industrial manufacturers. It was nothing like the game-day atmosphere he thrived on. Once Bubba got to an organization he really cared about, he crushed it. Imagine how much happier he would have been in his early career if he had sold based on his passion.

It's painful to launch yourself down the wrong path and try to change later. At that point, you've invested time in relationships and learned a lot that may no longer serve you. Most salespeople, including myself, were just looking for a good first job. There's nothing wrong with that, but you'll be better off if you take the extra time to find the best first job for you instead of just a good job in general.

Take a student who graduates from Ohio State University in Columbus, Ohio. She does an on-campus interview and is hired by a shipping company. Great pay, great training program. She completes the training and starts earning a good salary right out of college. It's the best management job she could hope for—but the job is in Camden, New Jersey.

She sets sail on her career selling cargo out of Camden. Now she's trapped in a concrete building staring at a computer screen all day and hates her life. Guess what? If this kid had taken the Kolbe A assessment, she would've known she didn't belong in Camden. New Jersey winters are too cold for her, and she doesn't like inside sales—or logistics—for that matter.

This happens all the time. People pick their careers from a limited pool based on what seems to be the best option. That strategy might work for a temporary job to pay the bills, but when it comes to your career, start with the ideal. Or at least the "Grandma Pick." That's what I call a job that your grandma would be proud of you for accepting. If it's good enough for Grandma, it's good enough for me.

Because the Kolbe A test told you what a great career looks like for you, you can search for a job that matches it. For the rest of your working life, you'll be happy. And because you love your job, you'll be a lot more successful at it.

Chances are, if you're passionate about something, there's a business that sells it. What if our Ohio State grad loves playing guitar? She plays gigs on weekends and spends all her free time practicing new licks and writing her own stuff. Instead of moving to New Jersey to sell shipping (or to New York to play on a street corner for pennies), she could've moved just outside Columbus to Dublin, Ohio, one of the nicest suburbs in all the Midwest. She's passionate about guitar, so she has a strong chance of getting hired to run sales at a local guitar manufacturer or other music industry business. She may not earn as much as the New Jersey gig, but with the cost of living being so much lower in Ohio, it would even out. If you're lucky enough to have a passion in your life, do whatever you can to sell it. If you love the weed business, go ahead and move to Colorado or Oregon to grow and sell it legally. If you want to get into the movie business, move to Hollywood. Endeavor to sell something that you already care about before you get into sales.

Now watch out for this head trash: "I love tennis, but after play- ing in college, I'm not good enough to become a pro, so I'm going to switch to logistics." You may not make your career as a pro tennis player, but if you love tennis, you'll be far better off working for a company involved in the tennis market. Look them up and talk with them about what jobs they have that match up to you.

Hot tip: It REALLY helps in your initial conversations if you have a story and know exactly what you're looking for. Say something like, "I play on the USC tennis team and will graduate next May. I want to stay in tennis, so I'm calling, trying to get a job in tourney promotions. I'm willing to travel anywhere." Your story and enthusiasm will be genuine, which will set you apart from other salespeople who don't care. You'll beat them to the sale just about every time.

If you know exactly what you want, you've already covered the hard part. Finding a great fit will be easier than you think.

The only way to align yourself with the right company is to do as much research on them as they'd do on you. If you worked for them, where would you be working? In a dark basement or next to your favor- ite park? What sort of people would you be interacting with every day?

How would you need to dress? If you hate wearing ties and staring at a screen, don't apply for a fancy corporate office sales gig!

And if you've already got a job, don't stop networking for other opportunities. In a perfect world, you should have two backup job prospects. You never know when a company could falter through bad management or another pandemic.

Let's pause here to take out some more head trash: "It's not what you know, it's who you know." This is a horrible myth many believe. Because you know me, I can get you an interview with someone who's hiring, right? Yeah, I probably can, but that doesn't mean you'll get the job. During the interview, you'd better know what you're talking about and have something to offer beyond knowing the friend who recommended you!

## GET YOURSELF ON A CAREER TRACK

Billions of people will be working during your lifetime. How many will be rock solid and living with purpose? How many of them are sales noobs in a non-ideal job, trying to figure it out before life gets away from them? I'd rather they figure it out now than two decades later. It is always possible to change course and figure things out. It's just far easier the younger you are.

People always try to catch me with an exception and ask about Colonel Sanders, who became successful when he was 63 years old. I'm not saying it's impossible, but the exception proves the rule. It's so much easier if you figure it out early. There's that little sweet spot when you're still going to college (or are just out of high school) and can start sorting things out by making some crucial first decisions. But once you get married and get settled in a job somewhere, you can't undo all that very easily.

How many people really drop it all and move to South America? Not many. It's important to get yourself on the career track sooner rather than later, doing what you're interested in. If you think about game theory and consider yourself the main player in this game, what moves would you make at age 20 to maximize your chances of "winning" the game when you're 30, or 40, or 50? Think that question through when you're setting up your first gig.

## A Reminder: Play to Win the End Game

Now that you have a handle on how to find the right job, let's revisit what you're working for.

I want to warn you again that as you accumulate commissions based on what you learn from this book, you may be tempted to buy a vacation home or an expensive car. And I repeat: Don't overextend yourself. I've seen many salespeople upgrade their houses, cars, and hobbies more than their commission checks allowed. They're not working toward anything. If you're not working for your freedom, you're doing sales wrong.

Freedom could mean a lot of things. Financial freedom means you never have to work again. Save for the assets that will earn you money rather than waste it. I never understood that when I was younger. Learn from my mistakes and save for your freedom now. No matter how perfect a job you find, wouldn't it be nice not to have to do it anymore? Play it cool until you hit your target. Tell yourself, *I am not buying a new car until I get this amount in the bank.* Easier said than done, but if you stick to it, your 30-year-old self will thank you.

We've traveled far in this book already, and you're ahead of your peers now. But the best is yet to come. The next five chapters focus exclusively on the sales profession itself, from meeting prospects every day to negotiating them into win-win deals, and from leveling up your sales skills to hiring your own team.

The format is a bit different from the chapters you've read so far. I've structured all advice into "What Not To Do" sections based on hundreds of interviews with six- and seven-figure-earning salespeople. I asked them what they wished they'd known earlier and what they wish they hadn't done. The insights in Chapters 4 through 8 are a direct result of those conversations.

Let's dive right in.

# CHAPTER 4

# YOUR DAILY PROSPECTING ROUTINE

**D**aily prospecting is the meat and potatoes and bread and butter of sales. It's the biggest boosting activity you can engage in. Making calls, following up, making calls, following up. But it's not always so simple.

There are plenty of mistakes that even experienced salespeople make. A sign of "the noob" is lots of activity and little results—but we're going to help shortcut that stage of your sales career.

By pointing out these mistakes, you can skip the struggle and do what works from the beginning.

Here we go.

## Fourteen Prospecting Mistakes Noobs Make (That You Don't Have To)

### 1. SKIPPING YOUR HOMEWORK

I recruited Gene Hindman as an intern when he was a college junior. He looked like he was still a kid, about five-foot-six and only 110 pounds (maybe). But Gene was tough as nails and determined as a bulldog. Fast forward 20 years later, he's a major in the South Carolina National Guard after deploying twice to Operation Enduring Freedom. He also manages merger and acquisition projects for one of the top human capital management providers.

I don't think anyone (except for maybe Todd Lorbach) made more calls than Gene. In retrospect, I wish I knew more about refining the list back then. We all made a ton more calls than we needed to and very likely went too fast on some of the important ones because we were trying to call so many.

It's not all about who's next in your database or who's next on your call list. You must take the time to identify the correct person in the correct market. Do they have the need, budget, timeframe, and authority? Miss any of these and you'll waste time with the wrong person. Once you have a well-practiced script, you should have a mentor (or someone else who knows what they're doing) listen to you practice your early calls to make sure you're doing a good job. It's like fishing. If you don't know what you're doing and think the goal is to see how many times you can throw your line out there, you'll cast awkwardly, throw the wrong bait, or go to the wrong place. You'll never catch anything. Or if you did, it would be pure luck.

As Gene gained experience, he got wiser about who he called and the approach he used. Part of this approach meant having an adult-to-adult conversation, and it's perfectly OK if the other adult doesn't need what you've got. The call is actually a discussion to determine that match. When we all started, we thought we were going to talk the other person into buying or make them buy because they liked us. Wrong.

Don't just dial for dollars. Dial for the right dollars!

## 2. MR. BOOK—MEET MR. COVER

You want to do your homework on your prospects. You want to know whether you're dealing with the equivalent of Joe's gas station or

Amazon. And you don't want to look stupid. We've all been stupid from time to time when calling a client. The dumbest thing I ever did when calling leads one day was ask, "What do you all do there?"

He responded, "It's the Internal Revenue Service." Sure enough, it *was* the IRS. I probably should have taken 10 seconds to look at who I was calling. I literally did not even take 10 seconds to look, I just dialed. You want to do your homework.

Once the prospect is qualified to be in your basket of people, your approach should be the same for all of them.

We don't know what a prospect's situation is until we talk to them. Joe's gas station could be a make-believe company, and Joe could really be running a big enterprise. Also, it could be a company as big as Home Depot, but maybe there's a small opportunity within the com- pany. Or, it could be a relatively small, unknown company with a huge opportunity. You do not want to judge a book by its cover. You want to treat all companies the same when they're prospects—just follow the normal process until you find out what the situation is.

On the other hand, keep in mind that the prospect is going to judge you based on several factors. They will start with the way you sound and/or look. I hear this often from noobs: "I called 14 people today; 10 of them hung up on me, and the other four said they weren't interested. Maybe I got bad leads." The truth is that you don't sound or look right. Maybe you sound timid; you're talking too slow or too fast, or you need more practice with someone who knows what they're doing.

Don't worry. Almost everyone starts out sounding bad. It takes practice and repetition. If you make 20 practice calls with various fake prospects, you'll move the needle in a good direction quickly, espe- cially if the calls are with a representative or manager who has made those calls hundreds of times. It's the same with your look. A mentor can help you get your look just right. You want to look professional but not too fancy. Be the relaxed pro in how you look and sound.

It's a tough balance to find. You may not want to judge others, but you're going to be judged based on how you look and sound. Even the way you write and what your emails look like will be judged. I might be representing the best product in the world, but if my email is too long, no one's going to read it. If it's in a bad format or the font is too small, it will be deleted. The same thing goes if it's too short. Something like the following is rude: "Bill, I do sales consulting. Let me know if you're interested, John." That's too short.

All these things have to be just right. I don't mean perfect. I mean 80 percent right. Writing a short paragraph of two or three sentences, dressing in a collared shirt and crisp pants, and sounding practiced and comfortable on the phone. Just enough so that you don't rub prospects the wrong way, but not so much that you're trying too hard.

Prospects will judge you by your cover, but don't judge them by theirs. This seems like a double standard, but it's a secret to success. It stops you from blaming others and helps you learn to do better. Another example of head trash? Telling yourself that someone was a bad lead or they must have been having a bad day. Then you look at your long, wordy email and think, *No, noob. It's because your email was too long. That is an auto delete.*

Maybe you're talking all the time, or you smell, or you need to shave off your pornstache. Not everyone should look like Colonel Sanders (though I tried that, and only the Colonel can pull it off. You can see it on my website at www.SchoolForNoobs.com).

Work on every aspect of your appearance, and don't be afraid to ask your mentor or boss for feedback. Once you find the sweet spot, it's easy, and your wardrobe can be quite simple.

# 3. MAKING TOO FEW CALLS

Making enough calls requires consistent effort. A noob mistake sales-people make is finding reasons **not to do it**. Then, when they're asked how many calls they've made so far, they say they haven't made any yet because they're working on a big proposal, or doing homework on accounts, or nobody answered, etc.

Really? I thought you were going to talk to 20 people a day?

Twenty times five is 100 per week, and 100 times four is 400 calls per month. Over 12 months, that's almost 5,000 conversations. Five percent of those buy, which is 250 new buyers. That's how it works. With a good call list and a rep that is trained up and ready to roll, it becomes a numbers game.

Another excuse I hear all too frequently is: "Well, I had two calls, but one of them was a really long one that lasted an hour and fifteen minutes." How in the world does one call last an hour and fifteen minutes? You're not talking about the product; you're shooting the shit about the weather or college football. A noob doesn't know how to control the call and get to the point.

It's easier to do when you have your call guide in front of you and you're checking things off as you go. Once you get through the "Hey, hello, how you doing" first few minutes, switch into your adult voice and get down to business. If they start to peel away to a non-biz subject, use your adult voice and bring them back with a transition like, "That's interesting about the basketball playoff situation; by the way, I know I only have you for another 15 minutes. Are you good if we get back on the return-on-investment discussion we were having?"

There are lots of salespeople with call reluctance who make excuses about what time of day to call and when not to call. They don't call because there's a virus. Then when the virus is gone, everyone's too busy for a call. Or it's almost New Year's. Get out of that head trash and make the connection.

Often what a noob thinks is the wrong time to call (like right before a holiday) is actually a great time to call because so few reps are making calls then! Busy people like to get things done; they generally work well outside traditional business hours. Many meetings, in person or on Zoom, happen on weekends, at night, on holidays, etc. Your prospects have the option not to answer your text, or your call, or your email, so don't think you are intruding on their weekend. Send about twice as many requests as you think appropriate, and that's still not enough.

If a prospect really doesn't want to be bothered, they will tell you. In that case, at least you found a non-buyer and you can focus on the rest. Contact your prospect often until you get a decision, whether it's "yes," "no," or "not now; please contact me at a later date."

You want to look out for that mistake because there are so many ways people make excuses to not make the call, even when they've made it their main goal for the day. One of the big excuses is the "Busy Trap." They're busy. They've been on the phone all morning. They're busy, but not getting anything done. They're not doing page-long conversations with multiple people and trying to find opportunities where there's a good fit because it's not as comfortable to talk about sales as it is to talk about Clemson football. Or it's easier to talk about the product instead of talking about the business challenges being faced by the client.

Often the noob is comfortable in the discussions that are more childish and superficial, but less comfortable in the serious adult-like conversations that talk about real problems and money. Think like a good doctor. Doctors don't have much time for chit-chat. Mine spends about 30 seconds on non-important questions, then gets straight to assessing my problem. Use your adult voice and get down to business. You can actually say, "Ok, let's get down to business" when you are ready to transition to the grown-up part of the call. That cues you both to focus. Try it.

Before you start thinking about that monster deal in year one and year two, from the very beginning you need to understand what the possibilities are. If you're selling a $5,000 or $10,000 product to a manufacturing plant that's part of Frito-Lay, that's great. How big is Frito-Lay? How many sites are there? All this information is available in about five minutes. You can figure out the exact number in North America, and then find the global VP of their supply chain. If they really like it at one factory, couldn't they consider it as a global standard and at least have the conversation?

I see it all the time—the noobs that make the minimum calls per day every day don't stay noobs for long. Make the calls first, then do everything else. If you just do this, you will be thanking me for a long time. Send me a picture from the yacht!

# 4. GIVING PROSPECTS NO REASON TO TALK TO YOU

One of my protégés, Francois, recently started working for a company. They had a lead who worked as a marketing staffer for a $100 million-a-year company. Francois talked to the staffer, who told him, "We just wanted to look at what's out there; no big deal." Instead of giving up, Francois went online, figured out who the CEO was, and discovered he just wrote a book. Francois ordered the book, read it, and then emailed the CEO. He told him he enjoyed the book and what he liked about it. Francois received a response that said, "Thanks very much. I appreciate that you started a conversation."

Now he had at least engaged with the CEO. Francois found a way into the account from the top. I don't know yet what will happen with that account, but Francois has always found creative ways to start conversations, and he will continue to create results where others may have accepted the first "No thanks."

Look at it this way. You're a business person. Determine whether anything you offer matches up with what a prospect needs. Often, you're bartering with dollars, but it could be something else. I want people to know what they're offering.

Another layer is finding out what you can do to help. My friend Francois got to work with the CEO because he hit that button in his brain. The CEO spent some money and took the time to write that book. Francois liked the book, so the CEO wanted to talk to him immediately. Francois hit that third level. It's all about making the prospect want to talk to you.

And don't give your prospects reasons to avoid you. I've come across several terrible salespeople in my time. They didn't give me a reason to want to talk to them. In fact, they were so bad at their jobs that I didn't want to buy from them. They gave me reasons *not* to talk to them. They sounded bad, looked bad, smelled bad; showed up late, talked too much, wrote long emails . . . I could go on. Don't do any of that!

# 5. FORGETTING THE VALUE OF SMALL FAVORS

A lot of people think that it's awkward to do favors for people because it can feel cheesy or like bribery.

The smallest things can have a huge effect. But most people—I'm guilty of this myself—just show up and talk business. It makes a statement when someone takes the time to do a small favor, like sending a Wright State t-shirt or a Citadel hat. You're not spending enough money that it would create an ethical situation, but it's a thoughtful and personal gift. Not a $50 Amazon card, but something small. A $15 item or something for the break room.

What stops us is the head trash telling us this kind of thing is cheesy. I've learned it's just the opposite. Doing a small, thoughtful thing for somebody makes a big difference. You will witness this one day, if you haven't already.

You see your contact for the first time and they greet you with "resting prospect face." They are representing a business and they are ready to discuss something serious. If you bring them a thoughtful, small gift, or send them one ahead of time, you will see a different face. They'll open up a little. You will see the person's actual face, the person behind the job. You'll still need to get back to business mode, but going forward they will treat you a little better than the next salesperson who calls them. And they're really responding to the thoughtfulness as much as the gift.

I'll never forget the chocolate cake man. He contacted me and said he'd heard what we were doing at Datastream. He wasn't sure, but thought he might have something to help us. He just wanted to come by and talk.

He showed up with a chocolate cake and said he'd put it in the breakroom for anyone who wanted it. We didn't end up buying any-thing from him, but that was pretty cool and everyone remembered it. If he'd come back a second time, he'd have gotten a big smile from everyone. And smiles open doors.

Sometimes I bring cookies or something for the breakroom, some-thing that's been baked that day. Then the next time I go back, they remember me. It's a little thing, but it works. One of our sales guys said that's one of his tricks. And he's a big-time executive at Salesforce and has also worked with Oracle. If it works there, it'll work anywhere.

He says that if he's trying to get through to someone but they won't call him back, he'll find out where the person went to college and he'll send them a small care package: a t-shirt or a hat with a personal note. You could write, "Hey, I'd love to talk to you for 10 minutes. I thought this might help me get in the door." Or write something funny. Almost 100 percent of the time, the person will agree to talk to you for 15 minutes. All in, it costs 30 bucks. What's that compared to the commission from a big account?

Small favors are valuable and thoughtful. If you brought a company hat with the prospect's initials on it, or something else that you know is personal to them, it shows consideration.

There are other things you can do that don't involve food. Start with a certain amount that won't create an ethics violation, maybe $25. Sending a tchotchke with your company brand shows you're being thoughtful but you're not trying to buy the business. Give something that's specific to the prospect, or even better, something specific from your area. It could be something your area is known for, particularly if you don't live there anymore.

If I'm calling on someone in Ohio, I might bring some Moon Pies or pecans from South Carolina. If you're from Vermont, you could bring maple syrup. More often than not, I've chosen something from our region, something that they might appreciate. Something that is thoughtful and not too expensive. It changes the dynamic right off the bat. I don't think I've ever seen anybody take on a negative tone if you show up and say, "Before we get started, I brought this all the way from South Carolina for you."

It's a little friendlier. Sometimes, if three guys show up with briefcases, and they're wearing suits, and you're sitting at the table, it can be a hard moment. Battle lines are drawn. Gifts add a softening touch. It puts everyone in a friendly childlike state, happy to get a present. Then, get down to business and switch over to adult talk: "Now, getting down to business, I need to hear the situation. What's going on here?"

But they remember that brief moment of childhood happiness. You made their day. That shows up in the relationship. So, spend the time.

## 6. ASK QUESTIONS (SHUT YOUR PIE HOLE)

It can be easy to get flustered and talk too much, or talk about the wrong thing. In a typical conversation with a prospect, you should be talking no more than 25 percent of the time.

The client may appear to be interested in you as a person—where you're from, your company history, or your product. But what they really care about is the problem they are having and how it affects their business, the future of their company, and most importantly, how it affects them personally.

Your main job is to find out all this important information. From there, you can solve their problems, make sales, and actually help your client.

Take the time to get trained. Have someone listen in on a call or do a call with you. Set up a scenario where someone is watching you in action. Get their feedback on running your mouth so you can un-noob yourself.

Have your questions ready, ask them, take notes, and shutteth the pie hole.

## 7. ASKING TOO FEW QUESTIONS

Noobs don't ask enough questions.

You want to have with you a one-page list of questions. You want to know how the person is doing, what's going on, and how things are in Ohio. You can get through that in two minutes, then move on to what they would like to talk to you about—the purpose of the call and the problem you're trying to solve. Keep it a simple, one-page list of questions, and end by asking what they would like to do next.

That said, you're not meeting with prospects for hours at a time. All you need to know is if they have a problem you can solve—and whether they will pay to solve it. Always carry a shorter list of six or seven questions so that you can check them off as you ask them.     Most salespeople don't do this. They won't even do it when you write the list for them and put it in their hand. Most will complain that they couldn't get all the way to number five. Just ask the questions. Sales becomes easier if you simply ask the questions.

It also really helps to get with an old pro or your manager and role play these questions and answers. Do it 10 times, 20 times, or as many times as it takes to get you feeling comfortable. Try it with different people. Practice is key to staying comfortable when you get in front of the real folks.

And keep your cheat sheet with you. Doctors use cheat sheets, pilots use cheat sheets, so you can too.

# 8. CREATING EXTRA WORK

Busy work is a problem. People like to look and feel busy, but that doesn't mean they are being productive.

As a noob, you probably create extra work for yourself unintentionally. Simply making the mistakes we've been discussing can add problems that slow you down. For example, if you realize you talked too much during a call with a prospect and failed to ask crucial questions to learn their needs, what are you going to say when you talk to that person again? You don't know, so you'd better figure it out. What will happen if you talk too much and spend too much time on the phone or if you take a zillion notes that you need to go through, which are mostly irrelevant? Or if you spend an hour researching a prospect and then don't get them on a call?

When you're new, it takes a while to get the formula right. Getting coaching will save you time and help you learn from your coach's mistakes. Get help early and often, and don't be afraid to fail during practice.

# 9. FAILING TO KNOW YOUR NUMBERS

Too many noobs don't know how many prospects they've talked to. They don't know their closing rate, and they especially don't know their closing rate broken down by vertical, industry, or deal size. It's too much for them to be able to do a product-level forecast where they can't report, given the product in a specific geography and industry, "This is the number of MQLs (marketing qualified leads)." Ninety-nine percent of salespeople don't know how to do that, and they don't know why numbers matter.

It's a huge mistake to not know the numbers related to your own performance. How can you improve if you don't know what is measured or how you're stacking up? You can't manage performance if you're not measuring it.

I'm very intuitive, and I never would have done any of this process work if not for my partner Larry Blackwell. He was the majority owner and CEO of our company and my complete opposite in many ways.

Larry was a Navy officer with a PhD in engineering. I had a liberal arts degree and some sales experience—opposite backgrounds, but we shared the same goal. For example, I would tell him we just made a great sale. He would ask about the process we used to get it, and of course, I didn't know because I was doing things on the fly in the early days.

Thankfully, he forced me to create the process and then "write it down." He asked me once, "How can you create a training program to teach these young people how to do it?" That got me thinking about the importance of tracing my own steps.

"How many calls a day do we need to make?" He asked for metric after metric. "How many leads a month do we need from marketing?" Basic things. He forced all that to happen. I never would have done it on my own. Though dealing with an engineer was sometimes painful for an intuit like me, together we figured out the process that worked for us.

On the other hand, process tracking can go too far in the other direction. Even some of the bigger companies get a little crazy tracking every "touch" of a prospect's record. To a large part, this will be out of your control, and you'll need to follow the process at your job. For yourself, just keep an eye on how much tracking is helpful versus how much is too much and unhelpful. You will get to make that call one day.

One metric that works in every field is how many conversations a day are you having with decision makers about what problems they are having and how you may be able to help them. From that number comes a certain number of proposals and then a certain number of sales, the most important metric being the first. Without that first conversation, there is no proposal and no sale. As they say, you must be present to win. Show up, make the calls, and have the conversations.

As of this writing (the end of 2020) several of our friends and Datastream alum have developed a product that lets you do most of your communications with your customer relationship management (CRM) through your Apple Watch! Check out yesflow.com and see how they are doing. That's Maxwell Smart-style. (If you're young, you may need to YouTube that reference, but Maxwell invented the shoe phone about 40 years ago.)

As mentioned earlier, I am a big fan of tracking how many legit conversations per day a sales rep has with possible buyers. They could be customers or prospects. You're just asking what's going on in their world, simply having conversations with people who could be buyers to see what's out there. You'll find a percentage of them do have a problem. You'll want to learn about that problem and turn it into a proposal or a sale.

Knowing your numbers is important. In some places, salespeople will be told what their numbers are. They'll use Salesforce or a CRM that tracks enterprise resource planning and CRM.

I work with plenty of people settling in at new jobs. They ask me, "How many people should I contact?" My standard answer is, "Your new manager will have good stats on this for your market. Follow what they tell you and try to do a little better than the average."

If you can, have a few legit conversations an hour where you are moving the needle forward or disqualifying the current opportunity. This is usually a pretty good process. Again, it will change based on different companies, but the best I have seen in terms of efficiency was a rep who started his day early, around 5:00 a.m., and went through the list of 150 prospects that were in his database. He'd find something of interest in the industry news and send his prospects a short email with the bit of info and request to talk later about it. Or he'd ask if they wanted to discuss the product he'd been reviewing.

He'd usually get 15 out of the 150 ready to talk that day because he caught them at the right time. He would set those calls up throughout the day and do it again the next day. He used a short, personalized email, sent it often, and tried to stay in front of them so that when they had a problem, they thought of him right away.

Tracking your numbers usually takes less energy and time than people think. And it's better than screwing around all day, which is what you'll do if you don't know your numbers.

## 10. LETTING YOURSELF BE IGNORED

Being ignored is part of the sales process.

Many prospects won't call you back or answer your email. This is their way of saying "leave me alone" or "it's not the right time." Noobs don't usually handle this well. They either get defensive or blame themselves. It's easy to write someone off when you are ignored or assume you somehow screwed it up.

The noob mistake here is to assume the worst. To think that the prospect must hate you, or maybe they bought from someone else. Before you ditch the lead, you need to understand that you're a small part of the prospect's world. They have other projects they're working on and other issues (both personal and professional) stacked up on their desk. They may love your product but have three other problems that need to be resolved first. Sure, it's a shame they won't just tell you that, but often (especially in the South) they won't say what they're thinking (bless their hearts).

When a good prospect goes quiet or dark on you, the best response is to put them on a 90-day callback list. In three months, try them again and act like nothing has happened. Just re-engage where you left off.

"Last time we talked, you had this situation; how's that going?" Requalify where they are. If it's still not a problem, just keep doing that every three months. You never know when the timing is going to be just right for them, and you want to be there when it is.

One noob mistake is to push too hard too early in a sales cycle, then give up when the prospects slow down. Don't do that. Play it cool, Luke.

We've started talking about the habits of the best salespeople, and the basics of working the process to become an expert in your field. This book is for noobs, so here's a basic reality check:

You might find you're coming in late. You're taking long breaks. You're talking to your girlfriend or boyfriend. You're having these long conversations with prospects about Georgia Tech football (Graham Strohman). You're making all these stupid new mistakes, but you're doing all right. You still have your job. You're above 50 percent. You're not in the bottom half of the sales team. And next year you're going to do better because you'll have been there a whole year and have some established customers for repeat business.

All of a sudden, you're doing OK. When that happens, many people start to think, *Leave me alone, pal. I don't want to hear it.*

The reason you get away with that, at first, is mostly because you're competing with other people who are just as noob as you are. But there's always that one salesperson who is just kicking ass. And everyone starts whispering that the performer got lucky or they got the good territory. In reality, they're doing the work and sticking to the process.

The difference between the noob that does everything right in the first year versus the noob that slides a little will be noticeable—but not crazy big. Not at first. What you need to understand is that the habits you build early on will stay with you over the next 10 years. That is when you see the noobs separate. One is still struggling or just getting by, and the other is already a sales VP and on a path to run a company.

The easiest time to establish that pattern in yourself is right now. As time goes on, anything is still possible, but it gets harder and you're less likely to change. Do it now.

How do you make that happen? What's the secret? What's that one word that if you say it, it turns the "no" into a "yes" on a dime? What do salespeople do that's supposed to be flashy, cool, sexy, and marketable? The reality is, it's not one big thing. Instead, it's committing to a lot of little things. Focus on the smaller aspects of your career, build those healthy habits, and they'll carry you to success.

## 11. Chasing Hundreds of Prospects (Instead of Dozens)

A lot of noobs believe if you call 100 companies, three to five might be receptive, and eventually, one will buy something. It's a pure numbers game played out over hundreds of fruitless calls. This only leads to burnout, and I'm talking in the short term. There are smarter ways to target a smaller number of accounts and cultivate higher-quality interactions with each of them.

How do you do that? How do you get over the fear of going from hundreds of prospects down to a few and putting all your eggs in those baskets? That's something you're not supposed to do, right? Start by realizing that when you invest in quality relationships, you're going to have better results.

Let me tell you a story. We give people IQ tests when we hire them, and Brian Edens was above the band that we normally hire. We almost didn't bring him on because he was too smart—that was my own head trash at the time, by the way. I figured that supersmart people don't last long in sales jobs. You're not going to keep them that long. They move on. But we hired him anyway.

Today, Brian is a killer software sales guy. In fact, he's a sales manager with IBM now. He's working with the largest companies in the world, dealing with green technology and big numbers.

When Brian started, he was one of the first of our sales reps to figure out this puzzle: If you have 100 leads, rank them by company size.

He'd consider, "What is the enterprise value of each company?" Joe's towing service is not going to buy anything significant from you. Brian would rank them that way. Then, before he called to ask a bunch of questions, he did a good job of determining what the problem was and how we could solve it. What would that solution be worth? This is not that hard to do mentally. It just takes time to figure out. Brian helped us all figure out where the money was!

Some salespeople find it extremely difficult to understand what the problem is that their prospect needs solved. For enterprise software sales, that's the only question that matters because enterprise soft- ware is about solving big, expensive problems.

Brian was one of the first people to figure that out. His method was to think about which accounts he should spend time on and how he could help them address their problems rather than making a purely transactional call. Brian used his adult voice and asked specific questions to get to the point and find out who needed help and who didn't.

Noobs often avoid this ultra-important question because noobs typically have head trash that says, "Sell every deal." By asking hard questions, more often than not, they'll find out there's no deal to be made. The quicker noobs can figure out this conundrum and deal with it, the quicker they will move beyond Noobdom!

Do not blurt out whatever comes to mind. Sales must be done subtly, with the message that "You're in this together." Say, "If it's OK, I want to ask you some questions to address what the big picture looks like so we can see where we can get to today." Assure them you're on the same page and want to figure out how to solve their problem. Most buyers don't know how to buy. This is another great area to do practice calls with a mentor and get comfortable having these adult conversations.

In the last couple of years, one of our original reps, John Harrison, told me about a monster deal he sold to a $4 billion-per-year hospital system. They needed the product badly and definitely had the money, but would not pull the trigger.

Being a hospital system, it was literally a life-and-death situation, but they couldn't figure out how to get it approved through the big IT system. John did a lot of questioning and listening, and finally figured out that what they needed was a full return-on-investment (ROI) analysis. But everyone on staff was so busy they simply couldn't get it done any time soon. John went ahead and did the work for them and got the deal. To solve their bigger problem, he had to identify and solve their smaller problem first.

Take the time to help the customer figure out what THEY need to get what THEY want, and help them get it done. Then, your deal gets done. If you can develop trust with the company you are dealing with, that allows them to open up and tell you the truth, and you'll succeed beyond your wildest dreams.

Become a trusted resource by knowing what you're talking about and truthfully trying to find out the best way to help a prospect—even if they don't buy anything from you at the moment. The next time you call, they'll remember how honest and helpful you were, and they won't give you the cold shoulder they give everyone else.

## 12. COMMITTING TIME SUICIDE

The amount of time wasting that happens in life can really add up. Suicide, when someone kills themselves, takes away whatever years they had left. If the person was 50 years old, they just gave up half of their 100-year lifespan.

If you are 20 right now and half-ass it for a few years, then you are time-suiciding a few years off your life. You're just shaving the years off now instead of enjoying the fruits of your hard work sooner. What's worse, you'll lose your most energetic and productive years and be forced to make up for them when you're older.

Most people fail to realize when they waste time doing something that is not deliberate, not in line with their goals, they're literally killing time. They're goofing off. They're not trying to enjoy life, have an adventure, or learn something. I don't know what's right or wrong for everybody, but as I have gone through my 20s, 30s, and 40s, and now into my 50s, I don't regret anything I have done. I only regret opportunities that I passed on. One example: I once was invited to a wedding in Morocco that would have taken me behind the scenes with interesting people from around the world. I passed because I was busy. Now I think back and ask, "What was I busy doing?" I have no idea. I should have gone to that wedding and figured out later how to handle whatever it was I was doing.

When your chances come, stop killing your time. Just go!

I've coached a lot of young sales teams over the years. They've always almost needed help in life management. I'm not talking about work time; I'm talking about LIFE time management. The personal stuff. At your age, it is hard to believe that time goes by fast. I encour- age everyone to be aggressive in how they take on life. Never settle for "normal" just because it's expected.

I've seen many folks waste life time by letting fear talk them out of taking any chances. I had a rep come to me once with a sheepish request for time off to compete in a Survivor-type show. I loved the idea, gave him a high-five, and assured him his job would be safe whenever he wanted to come back. Our company held team parties to watch him compete whenever the show came on. He did well in the competition and came back a stronger sales rep because of the experience.

Our company has also had reps leave to try other interesting opportunities, things like international relocation or dotcom stock options. We always sent them off with no hard feelings. Our message has always been, "Go for it and come back if it makes sense." Many times, they did come back and were stronger for the experience.

I believe everyone should weave in a trip around the world as soon as they can. It takes less time and money than you'd think. And the experi- ence and confidence you gain from the trip will help you graduate from Noobdom faster. Many of our young reps took the chances we offered them for international relocation to places like South Africa, Spain, the UK, Mexico, Australia, Singapore, Argentina, Canada, Holland, France, and Germany. Every one of those former noobs is crushing it today in international business/sales at places like Oracle, Salesforce, Infor, and Koch Brothers, and several have their own companies.

One of the former noobs, Todd Lorbach, took a job as a roving inter- national sales developer—our own Johnny Appleseed—and was out of the country so much that he didn't even have a full-time place to live. Todd the nomad was on the move for two years! At the time, the position was ill-defined, not super well-paid, and had an uncertain outcome. Needless to say, the position introduced an element of danger in his life that didn't exist living a "normal" life. He was 25 when we offered him the job, and I'll never forget, I had to call his wonderful mother, Sally, to explain what we wanted him to do! Can you imagine the experience and head start he got in business by taking that bold opportunity? Todd did business in over 60 countries and now does investment banking out of Dallas, Texas.

Have you lapped the globe yet? Here's an assignment, whether you take the trip or not: Go ahead and plan it out. Figure out when you want to leave and come back, which direction you want to head in (east or west), where you want to make your stops, who you want to meet, where you can stay for free, what you want to learn, who you want to meet, who you want to interview with while on the trip.

Here's another tip for you: The power of showing up. Let's say you majored in sports marketing, but you're not sure where to look for a job. How about reaching out to sports team owners around the globe who want to reach the US market? You could be a correspondent to introduce Australian rules football, Cricket, Darts, Snooker, etc. At the very least, you'll increase your experience in sports marketing. And who knows, maybe you'll find a really cool opportunity.

The main idea here is the *power of showing up*. It's one of the most crucial skills, and it almost always brings results. No one knows who you are until you make your presence felt and reach out to take your shot. This can be as simple as firing off an email that says, "Hi there, I'm from Kansas, USA, and will be traveling through Australia studying your football market. I am in sports marketing in the US and looking to learn and network. I am going to be in your area the week of xxxx; could I come meet you and see if we can possibly help each other somehow?" Show up, plan the trip, take the trip. If you can't even plan the trip, get used to where you are right now because you won't see much movement.

Pretend you are the 50-year-old version of yourself passing back in time just this once to talk to 20-year-old you. What would your 50-year-old self tell you today?

Speaking for myself, I would tell 20-year-old me a few key lessons:

- Look at each day as a new opportunity to enjoy life.
- Improve yourself with education and travel.
- Be kind to others (most are quietly hurting).
- Focus on today. Dwelling on wins or losses, yesterday, or what might happen in the future only distracts from today's actions.
- Get your priorities in order AFAP (as fast as possible). You will find health and family at the top.
- When it comes to business, the most important thing isn't just to "make money," but to become really good at what you do. If you are in the top 10 percent in your field, money will never be a problem.

And one last thing, a big one:

- If you save 10 percent of your income in a 401(k) starting when you get your first job and never touch it, your 50-year-old self will be very thankful. Same goes if you are into real estate. I have never seen someone buy one property a year and lease it out that is not rich, without a need for outside income in 20 years.

The point here is to start thinking about what YOU will be like at 30, 40, and 50, and decide what actions you can take today to be kind to your future selves. You'll thank yourself when you get older.

## 13. ONCE YOUR SALES AREA IS PRODUCING, YOU HAVE YOUR FEET ON THE GROUND

Once you build a flow for dealing with active customers and projects, qualifying brand-new leads, continuous sales, and product training, your days will become busy. It is easy and very common at this point to live in the "busy trap," to stop your proactive "sales fishing." This is a danger zone. Many noobs get happy here and stay "advanced noobs" instead of growing beyond this place.

The very best salespeople, the ones who push past the "feet on the ground" phase, are disciplined about prospecting and proactive calls. They continue to create a pipeline. A best practice is to have a specific time every day when you do at least an hour of pure business development (searching for new opportunities) in addition to the duties of handling current customers, prospects, and all the other non-revenue parts of sales life.

Keeping up your growth shouldn't take all day or even half a day. It's not about killing yourself with the speed dialer. It's not something random you engage in now and then. It's not solely for when your pipeline is depleted. It's every day at a certain time, with just enough time invested for your business to keep moving forward.

I have seen results from as little as one solid hour of this kind of calling a day. Consistent effort like this brings 10x better results than a rep that runs out of prospects and makes a ton of calls, then has customers and makes none, then runs out and makes a ton of calls again. Building a daily process towards your targets is key. Instead of referring to this as cold calling, choose something more positive, such as BizDev or business development. You're seeing if there's anything you could help a new prospect with. You're checking to see how things are going with customers and prospects, and you are fishing for new problems, referrals, sister companies, etc.

If they are all good to go, then you have done your job. Many times, they will let you know that so-and-so problem happened and they could use some help. In either case, with this low-key call, you win. If they are happy and don't have any problems, then you have checked on them and they appreciate it. If they do have a problem, you are ready to help them fix it! Now that's selling!

## 14. DOING WHAT EVERYONE ELSE DOES

You need to always be finding new ways to get in front of prospects and begin conversations.

Imagine you're a prospect and you receive calls from five different salespeople, all beginning exactly the same way. Boring, right? New approaches help differentiate you from everyone else. Don't be afraid to push hard, and maybe even try some crazy ways to start up a conversation. If your persistence pisses someone off, it was not going to be a match anyway, so be happy you identified a poor match and move on to the next prospect.

Most noobs err on the side of trying not to bother prospects. They end up missing potential sales because they never call. It is easy to fall into the head trash and worry about bothering a potential buyer. This goes double for noobs who have to get past the age gap of talking to older, more seasoned prospects.

One of our noobs was just the opposite. John Fradella was another outstanding Citadel grad we interviewed on campus in Charleston. He used a no-nonsense, in-your-face follow-up approach as one of his main weapons for success—and he even used it ON ME! It set him apart. I liked John a lot, but his Kolbe personality profile test identified him as an off-the-chart, stubborn entrepreneur—not an ideal match for us. As I recall, the folks at Kolbe told us, "This guy needs to be his own boss."

Now, I like those kinds of people, but they don't match up to what we want from our salespeople. So, I politely told him, "No," with the reasoning. Right on cue, he told me that I would be hiring him, that he would be the number one salesperson, and that he would call me every day until I "gave him a chance." I was sure at that moment that I would *never* hire him. He didn't match up on the test; he also challenged my decision, which I didn't really like (I am stubborn as well).

Well, fast forward two months. John had indeed called me EVERY DAY with all manner of attempts to get "a trial run" or "a foot in the door" or "to start working for free." His persistence went on and on. Finally, after two months, two people quit and I had no one in the pipeline for replacements. I had territories sitting open. I decided to give Fradella a chance.

And wow! He did indeed become the top rep. And sure enough, he also left after a few years (as Kolbe predicted) and became a wildly successful entrepreneur. John now runs the most popular tourist site in Hawaii, Hawaiidiscount.com, from his beachfront home in South Carolina. John could be a case study on persistence, timing, and working to match up with your natural talents. He remains a good friend to this day, and he loves to tell the story about how he got hired at my company in his first and only job as an employee!

You can remain professional and still speak up to the person in power. You've probably heard that the fortune is in the follow-up. You can't call, drop by or write a note and then take a lack of response as a no. Don't think that because they didn't reply, you're bothering them, or they didn't want your offer. If they haven't told you flat out that you're bothering them, they might not have seen your contact attempt the first time. Until they tell you to go away, they haven't said no yet. Just because you're being ignored doesn't mean it's a no.

You don't have to leave a phone message every day. But follow up every 90 days until you reach a yes-or-no decision. Consider sending a thoughtful gift, as we've already discussed. Offer to meet them at a convenient time, suggest joining them for their regular walk or another activity where you can tag along. If you really want to meet them and feel super creative, find out what they do outside of work. Do they serve on a nonprofit board or have a hobby you can participate in? Many opportunities happen outside of the conference room!

Try a couple of these different methods every 90 days with your prospects who are not engaged yet. If you do it too often (like every week), you'll become a pest. I know a sales consultant (and now friend) named Walker McKay who tried for over two years to reach me to start a conversation. Every 90 days, I would get something from him: an interesting book, a voicemail, a handwritten note, an article, an invite to a seminar. Walker kept it fresh and interesting, and one of those touches (two years later) came when I was working on a sales issue that was driving me nuts. At that moment, I decided to engage, and Walker really helped me. In fact, I learned the 90-day rule from him!

If your prospect is not ready, try different ways to start the conversation every 90 days. You will eventually catch them when they need you! And isn't that the time, when they need you most, that you actually want to spend time with them?

# FROM NOOB TO PRO: SIX ADVANCED PROSPECTING TIPS

## EVERYTHING YOU NEED TO KNOW ABOUT CORONAVIRUS

Sales work during "the 'Rona" has provided a lesson in adaptability. Lots of sales variables are changing—some in your favor, and some against. With more employees working from home, things are less certain.
How can you get prospects on the phone when they're distracted by their kids? Talking to people over Zoom is becoming the standard, so there's much less travel. There's no commute. You can't see each other face-to-face for those personal meetings, but you can juggle more appointments in a day because video calls are faster than in-person gatherings.

You could make up a million reasons why the virus is going to screw up your sales. Nobody can see you in-person so you can't leverage all your sales techniques. Half the people are sick or are worried about sickness. There are all kinds of horrible things going on, so nobody wants to buy. Or everyone is too busy with extra work from all the changes.

These excuses are all incorrect. I have seen the new sales landscape with my own eyes. Unless they were involved in a business that shut down (which is horrible), the majority of the companies I've talked to have said it's better now. People are sitting in front of their computers with their phones, and they're very open to talking. Heck, some are downright lonely. They're not having as many internal in-person meetings, and they're not traveling.

Your prospects might be *happy* to hear from you. You certainly have something to talk about, which creates rapport and a chance to form a bond. In fact, you could be the first human voice they've heard all day. Another good thing: because we're not doing as much, people have more free time. Company softball games are canceled. We're not going out to business lunches. No more birthday celebrations in the breakroom. We, as salespeople, have more time to follow our daily ideal checklist. What's your day supposed to look like? You can get more done now.

As an example, I've been thinking about writing this book for a decade. I took it on when I figured out how much more time I had during this "advanced stay-at-home time." I turned my suddenly empty hours into productive time.

Regardless of what is happening in the world, the most important daily success metric is your prospecting—the act of finding new companies that want to have a conversation about how your company can help them. Try to schedule one or two new conversations per day. You might think that target is too low. But 99 percent of salespeople quit making those calls when their pipeline gets full. You start by prospecting, and as soon as you get busy, you stop. Nobody likes to prospect, so it's easy to say you're too busy because you're working all these deals.

This is a standard Noob mistake that you can avoid. Keep your prospecting time on your calendar every weekday. Schedule it early in the day so you get it done.

It doesn't matter how busy you are. The number one measurement of success is prospecting every day. Sure, it can be boring sometimes, but do it. Work through your list and find one person who is willing to schedule a conversation with you about potential new business. Find one new opportunity every day, and you will become the top salesperson very quickly. Two per day, and the company owner will offer you equity!

Another thing that people stop doing pretty quickly is seeking out training. Everyone is interested in training at the beginning of their sales career. Then they get busy and stop. They plateau at a certain level, and get comfortable competing against others who are doing the same thing.

Avoid this noob mistake. Get all the training you can from your company. Add some extra learning every day, either in your field or in sales in general. There are plenty of trainers out there with web material, and YouTube has more free material than you could ever watch. A little learning every day, even just 10 minutes, will go a long way.

# THE OPA STRATEGY

Another technique similar to leveraged prospecting is called the OPA strategy. OPA stands for Other People's Audiences. This is where you do podcasts and interviews, go into Facebook groups and on LinkedIn, and do Periscope live, Twitter live, Facebook live, or Instagram live with someone who has an audience. Whatever the media platform, there are places that already have a lot of engaged people who can become your audience.

I don't understand why salespeople don't do more of this. Wouldn't it be better to talk to 100 people twice a day? Leveraged prospecting involves public speaking, even if it's one person talking to 20 people.

In today's world, most of the cold calling comes from LinkedIn. People try to find folks in the right geography and the right industry. They try to connect to determine whether people want to have a discussion.

Times have changed. LinkedIn is now the low bar of prospecting. Leveraged prospecting is outside-the-box thinking to help you become well-versed in the industry. And you can pick up new ideas from the top movers and shakers in your industry. Most of the new people I have engaged with over the last two years as a new vendor or partner are people that I heard or saw on a podcast, a Facebook group, or a Twitter thread.

What are the leaders in your industry doing to stand out? Do that! And borrow their audience when you get the chance.

# PUBLIC SPEAKING 101 FOR SALES

Public speaking is a skill that allows you to leverage prospecting through podcast interviews, seminars, and presentations in your area of expertise.

You want to be considered an expert in your space. This helps with sales, but it also helps you switch companies without having to start from scratch because being well-respected means people know who you are. It's good to have some independence from your employer later on. You can gain this credibility and develop your public speaking skills by running workshops on your product, service, or industry and by giving interviews on your subject matter expertise.

However, there's no substitute for actually speaking in public. At the end of the day, you must have some repeated experience doing that. You can watch YouTube seminars for inspiration. Dale Carnegie has a good one-day public speaking workshop. Toastmasters is also valuable.

There are plenty of things you can do to get comfortable speaking to large groups of people. At family dinners, you can say you want to give a quick announcement. Say, "I want to thank everyone for coming. We're so glad Irena is here; she came all the way from Washington. We want to thank everyone who could be here today." That seems like such a small thing, but if you get in the habit of doing something, it becomes simple.

When you have a business meeting, start standing up and speaking. This makes it feel natural, and you'll become more comfortable speaking in front of others. Every time you have a chance to say a few words, take it. The more of that you do, the more comfortable you'll get.

Before I do a speech, I'll usually put a few people together in a room beforehand and bring lunch. Then I run through it one time and ask for their feedback. That helps me refine not only the presentation but also my on-stage behavior. You can practice these skills as much as you want. Invest time into this. Before he gave his world-famous speeches, Steve Jobs would practice 100 times to make it come across as simple, effective, and effortless. One hundred times!

You don't have to go that far. Everyone's different. I like to do just enough so I'm semi-familiar with the speech, but then I'll wing some of it. Everyone has their own preference.

It's important to know that your chances of being a top dog will go up by a large factor if you're the one in the group who is most comfortable standing up and saying something. You will become a leader and a better communicator, and the group will start to look up to you. Your chances for success increase when you speak up instead of just sitting there. Getting yourself some speaking opportunities and getting comfortable speaking in public is a surefire way to get out of Noobdom fast.

So, take some classes, practice on friends and family, and study tutorials on YouTube. Just do it!

# CHAPTER 5

# SALES CALLS THAT CLOSE

If prospecting is what gets you an audience with a potential customer, the sales call is where you put on the show—and, we hope, do well enough to earn a standing ovation.

In your case, that's a company purchase order, request for the contract, or even money exchanging hands on the spot. It's the sale. It's what you're here to do. And just like in prospecting, there's plenty that most sales noobs get wrong. In this chapter, you'll learn what doesn't work so that you can avoid mistakes, sell more, and get paid like a pro.

## Thirteen Sales Call Mistakes Noobs Make (That You Don't Have To)
### Assuming You're an Inconvenience

The biggest head trash for most noobs is thinking nobody wants to talk to you just because you're the new person. You might figure people think you don't know enough, which can make you have more call reluctance and less confidence on the phone.

Buyers can smell discomfort. Aim to sound like you're talking to a friend on the phone (with a loose script to follow).

A variation of this head trash is assuming that the new reps always get the bad leads or the bad territory. Sure, sometimes that happens. You may not get the *best* leads right out of the gate. Your job is to get supremely comfortable talking to people, following the guide, and having a genuine conversation about what your prospect is dealing with and whether you can help. Practice until you get comfy—then have the conversations.

On a side note, my company didn't give terrible leads to the new reps. But we would often assign them the Northwest (Washington, Oregon) because it was a little territory, and because no one really wanted to deal with the time change from the East Coast. As people did well in the Northwest and something else opened up, we moved them to Ohio or Florida or somewhere that was typically better.

That was my head trash, too, that the Northwest was a throwaway region and made a nice starter territory. What's in the Northwest? As it turns out, Amazon, Starbucks, Boeing, and a bunch of other great companies. My new reps could have made their whole living dealing with any one of those companies. Both Amazon and Starbucks eventually became our customers, but at first, we didn't pay them that much attention. Yes, they were smaller 20 years ago, but that head trash went all the way through to the owners of our company (my partner and me). We both put noobs in the Northwest and thought, *Who cares?* Three of the biggest possible accounts ever for our software were right there, and they were already customers, and we let it go to the noobs.

Why was the Northwest always just an okay producer for us? Because that is how we treated it. This story is proof that you can make mistakes along the way and still do okay. It's also a testament that whatever area you get assigned as a noob, you can find a way to make it produce!

# SOCIALIZING WITH PROSPECTS

Noob salespeople believe that it's really important to go out drinking and socializing with the customers. This line of thinking wrongly assumes that customers like to get drunk with us and have fun. Some assume that you will misbehave together and form some great bond.

We experienced salespeople did a lot of that. In retrospect, it didn't help. It also didn't kill us; we still did very well. But what it taught me was the relationship part of the sale should go only so far. You're exchanging value and trying to build professional trust. That does not require heavy socializing. You won't earn professional trust by showing prospects how many shots you can drink in a row. For a long time, I couldn't get out of this wrong way of thinking.

Most of my salespeople did the same thing. When we came to town, we took our potential customers to a ball game or we stayed out late, all so that we could say, "Yeah, I've got a great relationship with this guy, Woody, in Chicago." We'd have a party relationship, but we were foolish. The real relationship measurement should have been how much money we helped Woody's company save every year for the last eight years. We should have been looking at what kind of promotion path Woody was on, and what happened to his business as a result of our relationship.

That's how I think today.

When we were young, our head trash told us we had to butter people up with a good time and some drinks to get them to agree to a deal. That's how I noobed myself. Now I know better. Now I spend that time showing the customer how I'm going to save them money, and then I follow through.

Sure, I'll admit that sometimes you do end up being friends. And forming that dual relationship *can* work. It just honestly lessens your odds of success because it increases your risk of looking like a fool while you're drinking. And it wastes a tremendous amount of time.

Be smart. Err toward staying professional. Be more like the client's doctor than his college beer buddy. They'll respect you more.

# ACTING TOO CHUMMY

You want to build rapport at the beginning of a call, but don't get stuck there. Noobs will begin with small talk, but then they don't move on. They get stuck in "first gear." A lot of salespeople will say, "Ohio? My girlfriend's from Ohio. She went to Ohio U...." And they go on and on. Then when they do the call review, they assume it went really well because there was a personal connection! But when they're asked if the prospect needs the product or service, they don't know. They forgot to ask.

The other party will often let you ramble as long as the topic is interesting to them. You're not going to get prospects saying, "Listen, it's nice to meet you, and I'm glad you're from Ohio, but let's get down to business. I've only got 20 minutes, all right?" They'll let you ramble, then they'll hurry you off the phone because you're chewing up their time.

Unless you're just going to be pals, both parties should want to get somewhere. Think like a doctor. Nobody wants their doctor to be too friendly. We want to know what's wrong with us and how we are going to fix it. Small talk, problem, solution.

Stay focused on the purpose of the call.

# SEEING THE PROSPECT AS ABOVE YOU

Noobs often consider themselves to be a child talking to the adults. They step into a new industry where they don't feel confident yet, and they feel outclassed by seasoned prospects. They revert to trying to get the adult to buy their stuff like a child would, by being friendly and cute. You must move from acting like a child/college student/noob into an adult-to-adult relationship dynamic.

Make sure you're not overly concerned about making the sale, or making friends, or getting an adult's approval. You're there to have a conversation and understand their possible business problems. If there's something you can help with, great. If there's not, no big deal.

"Nice to meet you, let me know if we can ever help you, and we will stay in touch a few times a year."

Most salespeople start out putting a lot of pressure on themselves. A lot of sales managers make that worse because they're scared, they have to make their numbers, and they need *you* to make the calls. They are frantic, and you can hear it in their voices. Your prospects will hear it in your voice, too.

The best sales managers maintain calm even under pressure. That's where you want to get to. Cool and calm. Stop trying to prove yourself like a child and focus on your fundamentals.

## THINKING YOU MUST TRICK PROSPECTS

I'm the salesperson, and you're the buyer. I'm trying to sell you something. You'll be doing me a big favor if you buy from me. I have to coerce you, trick you, and do whatever I can to get that sale.

Right?

Wrong. Talk about head trash.

You have to transcend that way of thinking because it's simply not true. The truth is, you're both busy. You're each working for a business (or some type of entity) and you're looking to swap something. In many cases, it's dollars for a service or a product. But sometimes, it's a service for a product, or a product for a dollar.

Noobs often focus on the commissions they will make if a sale happens. A pro thinks about how the customer's business will benefit if they go forward with your product. If you can start thinking more about the value you bring than the potential commissions you'll get, the sales will roll in.

Always ask yourself, *What is my customer getting out of this deal?*

## Letting Your Conditioning Get the Better of You

If you ask a kid how school was, they normally say, "Fine."

89

When you walk into a retail store and they ask if they can help you, you reply, "Thanks, just looking."

Patterned replies can kill your sales business if you don't learn to manage them. You need to get better at having meaningful conversations. Instead of those standard types of questions people are used to brushing aside, ask them to tell you more about what they need. Then spend some time thinking about the opportunity. Pick one question that expands on that need and keep digging.

"Can I help you?" is a question we're all conditioned to answer in the same way: "No, I'm just looking." It's like call and response. "Marco." "Polo!"

I had a salesperson ask me a great question once: "What did you walk in here for today?" I didn't have a clever answer. I had to think about it. If you ask a better question in a better tone of voice, it leads to a conversation instead of a standard throwaway answer. Think about what they ask you when you walk into the Apple Store: "What are you here for today?" Not, "Can I help you?"

Figure out which questions are best for your business and ask them over and over.

To get away from that conditioning, no matter what your question is, learn to accept the standard answer without giving up: "We're good right now. We think we're OK with our current vendor." Then say, "As long as I've got you on the phone, would you be open to spending 10 minutes talking about your company and what you're doing? Maybe I can help you in the future if your vendor ever causes you trouble." Spend those 10 minutes getting a walk around and try to learn something.

Salespeople are often reluctant and nervous because they are scared of the answer. Sometimes when they hear the standard answer, they check that prospect off the list, thinking they're not interested. Instead of giving up, make an honest effort by letting your prospects know what you're trying to help them achieve.

Here's a personal example. When I was in my 20s, I drove a Saab. I packed my young family in the car and headed to West Virginia, where my in-laws lived. It was the night before Thanksgiving, and traffic was crazy. So, of course, my car broke down on a busy highway. I

Called the nearest Saab dealership, the Saab/Volvo dealership in Spartanburg, South Carolina, told them my Saab had broken down, and asked what they could do. The sales manager was helpful and understanding. "Yes, sir, Mr. Sterling. I'll tell you what. We'll send a tow truck to get your car; we'll send a car to pick up you and your family, and bring you back here. Then we'll work it out from there." Sure enough, they towed our Saab and sent a car for us, and I walked in to talk to him. I had my hackles up because I had this head trash about dealing with car people. It was a really lush-looking place, and when we met, he was a smooth talker. I expected a battle.

"Mr. Sterling, you've got a couple of choices here. Options are limited because it's Thanksgiving, but you're in luck."

"What options am I looking at?"

"I'm sorry to say I don't have a Saab for you, but I've got a relatively new Volvo station wagon. How long are you going to be gone?"

"Four days."

"No problem, Mr. Sterling. Why don't you take the station wagon while I get your Saab's paperwork. I'll let you use it. We'll call you about fixing your car and give you an estimate. If you're OK with it, we'll fix it, and you can pick it up on your way back."

We got a great Volvo for the trip, and we were treated like kings. We drove it there and back while the Saab was fixed. It was a perfect transaction.

The only thing he didn't do was put me in his follow-up system. In the old days, dealerships took who ever walked on the lot. If he'd put me in their system and kept me up to date on what was for sale, I don't think I ever would have bought a car from anyone else. He had a chance to help me, and he did; it probably didn't cost him a nickel. It was a borrowed car off the lot, but the personal touches made me feel like he gave me a Rolls Royce.

That's something important that I teach salespeople. When you have a chance to do something or deliver for a client, go all the way. Don't say, "We can get you the car, but you're going to have to sign this waiver for a million dollars, and we're going to need a thousand-dollar deposit on your credit card." If you're difficult about it, it's not going to work out. Don't go part way. Go all the way. Two important noob lessons here:

1. When you have a chance to help a prospect, go all out.
2. Don't forget to keep ALL of your old prospects in some type of follow-up system, even if it's just for your personal and business connections.

Here's a more recent example from the music world. I play sax for fun and am always looking for new gear to make me sound better. A company in France, Syos, has come up with a new sax mouthpiece made out of some kind of new resin. Their pitch is to have customers listen to the sound on the computer. They sell you on the fact that you pick the sound you like, send them the file, and they'll make the mouth- piece using 3D printing technology as close to the sound you choose as possible. It's unbelievable. If you get it delivered and it's not right, you tell them what's missing. If it's a little too bright or it sounds too dark, they'll make another one and keep sending you new ones until you're happy. If you're never happy, you get your money back. If you're not delighted with the best mouthpiece, you don't pay a dime.

It makes me feel good to have a company that takes care of me like Syos does. If you can take care of your customers like they do, you will crush it.

Another example of taking extreme care of the customer is a company called Pardot (owned by Salesforce now). They were early in marketing automation. They called me once to see if I was interested. The salesperson's pitch went like this: "I know you said you're looking at marketing automation. A lot of people are thinking about it right now, for sure. Here's how the Pardot model works: We charge $1000 a month per business enterprise. The first thousand is due in 30 days. If you don't like it between now and 30 days, don't pay the invoice. No hard feelings."

I asked, "What about the services?"

"All the services you want and need to get it installed and working for the first 45 days are included. We'll put a team on it, and if we can't get it done in 45 days, you don't want us as your vendor." He had a good answer at every turn, which kept me thinking, *This is a good deal for me. It's either a good deal or I'm out with no risk other than the time it takes to try it.*

Pardot eventually sold the business for $90 million to Salesforce.com. The pricing and the way they went about minimizing the risk to the prospect was a real claim to fame. I experienced it myself going through the sales cycle, and it stuck with me.

## SELLING TO YOUR COMMISSION

You must get past thinking that you're trying to get the prospect to give you $100,000. That's the bad way of thinking because it's all your way. You want to think just the opposite: How can you help your prospect?

You want to get Charlie to recognize that you're going to give him $400,000 of value in his business over two years. In return he's going to give you $50,000 this year and $50,000 next year. He's exchanging $100,000 over two years for $300,000 of added profit. That's the promise of value exchange.

Salespeople too often focus on how a $100,000 sale gets them 8 or 10 percent as commission. The quicker you can get beyond that money thinking, the better. Don't look at the dollar amount you are getting from your customer. Look at how much their business will benefit per year from working with you. If they believe that number, or better yet, see it year after year, they will have no problem writing you a big check every year. You're going to make more money long-term by thinking about their value than you will by only thinking of your own value.

Think about it this way: A million dollars is a big commission in any market. I only know a few people who ever got a commission check for over a million. But, if you were to prove to me you had a way to help me make $10 million a year, don't you know I would be happy to pay you $1 million? The more value you create for the customer, the happier they will be to pay you. The sales goal you want to strive for is one where you walk arm-in-arm with the customer in partnership down a path that makes money for you both. This is the opposite of fighting with a prospect over "getting" an order.

I made a lot of sales in the first 10 years. You will too, even if you don't fully understand what you're doing just yet. If you're thinking about selling, are making calls, and are pleasant and comfortable on the phone, you'll make some sales. But it's only when you crossover into thinking that you're going to help the prospect that you see the really big wins. If you can, tie the benefit of what you are selling to the business metrics that the owner tracks, track it all the way to the owner, and show how you are dropping their expenses by $500,000 a year, forever.

Don't ever say, "It's a no-brainer!" There are lengthier versions of the same tired push, and they usually sound something like this: "Our stuff's $400,000, and everyone liked the demo. We are better than the competition. We showed you three references, and we all like each other. We've got the best project manager picked out for you. What do you think? Do you want to do it?"

That is pushing, and most people resist and push back. Your job after finding a legit problem to solve is to help the customer figure out just how much their business will be affected financially if they have you solve the problem for them. You close the deal by proving to them you can solve it with demos, references, or a prototype. One of the best things (and fastest ways) to get out of Noobville is to get on the same team with your prospects. This is not a fight—It's a walk together.

## EXPECTING EVERY LOTTERY TICKET TO WIN

Sales noobs often tie their self-worth to what they do. Then they get upset when they don't make a sale.

I teach my students to think of it a different way. We all have eight people to call today. We have eight conversations today, and there's 10 members on our team. That's 80 lottery tickets. We all do the call exactly right with the perfect intonation, using our call guide, and we don't miss a beat. We do it right. Then we're going to get two sales. Two of these lottery tickets are winners. If we screw up half the calls, we're going to get only one sale.

During your daily calls, the only thing you can control as a sales noob is setting up your calls each day and making all your calls correctly.

That's all you can control. Whether it makes sense for the prospect at the moment, or whether they will give you the order, is beyond your control. We're not trying to pressure or trick somebody into buying. We're trying to see which scratch-off ticket is a winner—which call will be the sale. This takes the pressure off making the sale and puts more pressure on the process of having eight business conversations and getting them done. They don't have to be done perfectly. They have to be done 80 percent right.

When you understand that better, you take the pressure off yourself regarding these calls. I can remember as a young sales rep going into every call thinking, *This is the one.* Everyone on the team was ready to get in there, like a basketball game.

One of the central themes I teach people is that you need a consistent and reasonable number of business conversations every day. But if you're talking lottery tickets, the more low-pressure conversations you can have, the better your chances are to generate some success. You want to get your skills up to the reasonable 80 percent level.

Once you get to an 80 percent effectiveness level in sales, the key component comes down to how many business conversations you have every day. You turn your job from high-pressure to a cool numbers game. Remember, each call is like a lottery ticket. Don't get all weird about it. Heck, the call may be a dud; maybe they're not ready. Just relax into it, enjoy the conversation, and keep your ears open for when the prospect has a problem that they are willing to discuss solving with you. The best noob grads make their calls every day, listen like a good doctor, and find enough "winners" to be very successful. That's the formula.

Getting comfortable can be easier said than done, but when you develop that "relaxed caller" mindset, it becomes less difficult. It's also better if you reach a certain number of conversations every day. If you tell yourself you're going to work hard to have eight conversations a day, you can expect one of those conversations to set up an appointment. Six of them will tell you maybe in 90 days, and one of them will tell you to go to hell. If you get your numbers, you'll start to see a pattern, and you won't be surprised if somebody is rude every now and then. You also won't be surprised when someone says that you might be able to help them, and that they'd love to schedule a call.

If you keep playing the "lottery," you'll eventually get a winner. Keep scratching.

## FALLING INTO THE PRODUCT TRAP

During a sales call, when you have a little bit of rapport, don't fall into the "Product Trap." This is a common noob mistake that can happen when the prospect asks about the product. You've come this far, and they're interested in what's next.

Then you start describing the product and how it works, and you never get past the middle part. Suddenly you're yapping on and on about every feature and benefit. The prospect is listening, but their eyes start to glaze over, and they lose sight of the solution.

I coach people not to get caught in this tempting trap. Don't waste your prospect's time giving them two hours of explanation about the wonderful product. At least wait until you confirm that you have a good fit. Instead, I coach salespeople to push the technical part to get to the end of the sales cycle.

Noobs do a lot of demos. Noob grads do very few demos and only at the very end of the sales cycle as a final step before the order.

Focus on what matters to your prospect, and don't get bogged down.

## TRYING TO RELATE WHEN YOU CAN'T

You ask your prospect, "How's it going today?"

They reply, "It's been kind of a difficult day. I lost a foreman this morning so it's been really tough."

The noob tendency is to "top" the comment. "Really? I remem- ber when we lost our foreman two years ago. It was a real mess. That's painful."

That's false relating. You think you're relating, but what you're really doing is saying, "I don't care what you just said. I'm going to tell you about what happened to me and how interesting I am. In fact, I'm more interesting than your problem."

You must train yourself, as I have, to ask instead, "Really? Tell me more about that."

- What happened?
- Why did it happen?
- What can be done about it?
- What's the problem?
- What are the issues?

Do you see what this approach accomplishes? By doing this, you're showing empathy. You're making the prospect the star of the conversation, and you're listening for some area where you can help. This is a huge part of selling that only the top 20 percent of salespeople ever learn. The top 20 percent of doctors understand how to do this, too. But most people never realize this approach or why it's so powerful.

Escape Noobville—Stop topping your prospects' stories. They only care about their own stories, not yours.

I once coached a guy who had a college internship with us. When he called a prospect, he said, "Hey, this is Graham Howell, and here's why I'm calling. We want to find out whether this thing we have is worth your time and if you want to talk about it." That was the whole conversation. It was PERFECT.

Typically, a new salesperson will take that simple call and completely screw it up by over-talking. Their opening might get really long and flowery and full of big words that will turn the prospect off. If the salesperson is trained and knows how to make that introductory call, it doesn't matter whether they're 16, 26, or if they went to college. Either they can set up the call, or they can't. If you know how to do that when you're talking to your prospective employer, they'll figure it out quickly because you've got something they want.

Noob—When you are starting out, keep it short and sweet. Your prospects and bank account will thank you.

# TRYING TO CONVINCE PEOPLE TO BUY

I love the assumption that sales, as most people practice it, is convincing people to buy what you're selling. I love it because it's wrong, and it makes me laugh because I used to believe it.

Sales is actually about having a purposeful conversation to see if the prospect needs what you're selling. It's not just about saying the right things or manipulating people. Sales managers, myself included, used to teach noobs incorrectly to "overcome" objections. We would ask why the prospect didn't buy, and he'd say he wasn't ready right now because he's putting in a new piece of machinery or something. We would respond that we'd give him a free week of service and send the person out there to do it. If they said it's too much money, we'd let them pay for it over time. In this way, we were encouraging them to start putting pressure on the prospect.

This is not the right way to walk together. The old way is more like a battle.

Don't place unnecessary pressure on the prospect. Instead, make it clear you only want them to do it when they're ready. You want to make it easier for both parties. Sales life is easier when you don't feel like you have to make the sale (and when you have a big pipeline of other prospects). When prospects feel like you don't have to make the sale, that you're just trying to help them, they're more eager to buy.

Marketing note: If you get special offers or deals from your company from time to time, there's nothing wrong with casually letting the prospects know about them. Sometimes a sweetened deal makes the obstacles disappear. But to get past being a noob, don't fight with the clients—be on the same team.

# GETTING AWKWARD ABOUT MONEY

Most of us get two difficult beliefs hammered into us as children that make sales a lot harder:

- Don't talk to strangers.
- Don't talk about money.

These may be important lessons for polite society, but they don't apply very well to cold calling.

There are a lot of these head trash pressures to grapple with. When salespeople are tasked with cold calling, they have to deal with some of these negative thoughts while waiting for someone to pick up. If you're able to get someone on the phone, you might be worried you caught them at a bad time, or they might hang up on you, think you're being rude, or be upset you're interrupting their day. There's a lot of negativity for noobs surrounding a sales call.

I coach people on the other side of the noob fence to bring up the money early. Change your voice to an adult tone and say, "That's interesting. Before we go any further, are you OK if we talk about money for a minute to make sure we're on the same page about where we're going here?" Typically, their voice will also change, and they'll tell you to go ahead. You both change into adult mode and have a conversation that will probably go like this: "It's normally $200,000 a year for a company your size, and the typical savings is about 5 times that per year. Are we in the ballpark, or are you going to hang up now?" If they say that's fine, the tone goes back to being light and conversational.

Some noobs are awkward or apologetic about the price. It's almost like they're wincing because they don't want to risk spooking the pros- pect with a number. We've all seen salespeople who pitch their voices down when they mention the price. Then they add, "Or at least that's our starting price."

Your product or service is either worth the price you charge or it isn't. If you're saving the prospect a fortune compared to your price, you should believe that. And you should convey that value to your pros- pects when you share the price, not apologize for charging to help them.

# FAILING TO ASK FOR THE SALE

I've been in this situation a few times as a potential buyer. The salesper- son has answered all my questions. I like what they're offering, but they haven't asked me if I want to buy it yet. I can tell they want to, but they hold off. It becomes awkward.

Most prospects start out blank, and you try to lead them down the path to solving their problem because they don't know how to do it. Most prospects don't know how to buy, and many noobs don't know how to sell.

If you want to make it really simple:

1. ID your best targets (those that likely need your product).
2. Talk with them about what they do and what problems they have.
3. Every 90 days, contact the ones who aren't ready.
4. Ask the ones that have problems now, "Are you open to us proposing how to help you solve them?"
5. Treat the prospect as a partner in solving the problem.
6. When you talk about the money, also talk about "the order." "When do you want to have this solved?"
7. Ask about their payment system: "If you decide to go forward, how will you get the order processed internally?"

Sales pros are not afraid to risk killing their "pretty little pet"—the sale. They ask the hard questions early, even if that leads to a "No." Doing this makes them better partners to their customers, and that makes them pros.

# FROM NOOB TO PRO:
# THREE ADVANCED SALES CALL TIPS
## ANATOMY OF EFFECTIVE SALES CALLS

There are a few varieties of sales call templates with common similarities and differences. The purpose of a template is to simplify the process for you and create an easy-to-follow anatomy of a sales call script that you can memorize. That template tells you what you are supposed to do—what you say and in what order, from the beginning of the call through the objection handling—to get to an answer.

# THE OPENING

Most noobs screw up the opening by taking too much time. This is a quick, feeling-out time to make sure you both speak the same language and are agreeing (without actually saying the words) to have an adult, polite conversation. Spend no more than five minutes on the introduction and small talk. If you take less than a minute, it feels rushed. If at all possible, do not talk about yourself or try to top the other person's story. If they say they went to Clemson, no matter what, don't let that subject trigger you to "top" them with all of your Clemson stories and connections. Stay focused on them. Ask more about Clemson.

Here's an example of what not to do. I'll show you a too-common example of a non-smooth, McGroove noob.

Prospect: "Yeah, I'm from this area and went to Clemson. I played on the club basketball team for three years. We even won the University Cup during my last year. That is pretty much my claim to fame at Clemson."

Noob: "Wow, I went to Clemson, too; in fact, I've had 16 family members go there, and one is on the Board now, which is nice for football tickets. We are basketball folks, too. I played for the Tigers when I was in school back in the '90s, and Dad played back when they had Tree Rollins, and he went on to play a few years for the Lakers when Kareem was there; in fact, Kareem is my godfather! I didn't make the NBA but did play seven years in France. So yeah, it's cool to have Clemson in common."

The coolness of this noob's Clemson connection only makes the prospect feel like a loser and resent the noob for his cooler life. The prospect won't come out and say it, he just won't buy, and the noob will scratch his head and say, "But we had such a good Clemson connection!''

Remember: No matter what, the prospect is the cool one—not you. You will be cool later with your sales pro success.

## UFA

Once you get through your five minutes of polite chit-chat, you need to transition to the Up-Front Agreement (UFA). This is where you transition from your friendly voice to your adult voice. Speak slower and lower. "Hey, before we get started, let's go over our agenda for today and make sure we are on the same page, okay?"

Over the phone or using an actual or virtual whiteboard, list what you want to cover today in order and ask for their input. Agree to the items and expected timeframes. Don't forget to include agenda items to discuss money, what getting started together would look like, and next steps. It is easier to talk about the "hard stuff" if it is on an agreed-upon list. The UFA will change your life. Create one before any meeting or agreement, and you will get a ton more done and waste less time.

## MARVIN GAYE: WHAT'S GOING ON?

Once you have the agenda down pat, it's time to find out what is going on with them. "What's going on?" is a great open-ended question that allows the prospect great latitude in answering. If they need help, you can refine the question into, "Tell me where things are today for you and where you want them to be?" You are looking for a gap that you can come back and propose to solve. If there are no gaps right now, it is not the right time, and they go on the 90-day check-in list.

## AN EXAMPLE CALL

The anatomy of a software sale is similar no matter what the offer or industry. Let's go through a sample call together. This example Zoom call is with a manufacturing company prospect who saw something on a website that they liked about the salesperson's software. He's calling to get information about the product.

The salesperson opens with a friendly question (friendly banter).

"Hi, Dave. Where are you calling from?"

"I'm here in Detroit, Michigan, where there are quite a few manufacturing companies. We're one of the ones who've made it."

"I'm glad to hear it. That's good. I haven't been to Michigan in a long time. What's happening up there?"

"Well, a lot of places have reopened. Most of the companies that we worked for, all the vendors there, are back up and open. We've had quite a few orders come in. It's been a rush to try to fulfill all the orders, work with our suppliers, and let our customers know that things are going to be a little bit late. It's been hectic trying to adjust to the social distancing and mask rules. It's been crazy up here."

"You sound like a busy guy. Before we get going, let me ask how much time you have today."

(Transition to UFA)

"I budgeted about half an hour."

"Half an hour. That should be plenty. I think we'll probably finish before that. Now, you called me, Dave, so I want to make sure I understand. What is it that you want to get out of this call? What are you looking for today?"

"What I really want to know is how we can fulfill this backlog of orders that we've got. We have new customers coming in with big orders that are the best we've ever had if we can get to them. But from March through the beginning of summer, we've had so many orders come in we haven't been able to connect with all our suppliers. We need it streamlined. It's chaos on the floor. We need to get that fixed. I'm thinking that having improved software will be better than hiring someone to run through our spreadsheets and figure it out manually."

"OK. I'm hearing you want to understand what our software might be able to do for you?"

"Yes, I'm curious. I'm not quite sure what it does, but I think it might be a good fit."

"All right, good. I'll make sure we do that. And then, from my sheet of paper, I want to ask you enough questions, so I have an honest feeling for whether I'll be able to help you. Is that OK with you?"

"Sure."

"OK. Because I don't know yet if we can help you. I'll ask you questions about your manufacturing floor, just rough financial questions in terms of production and those kinds of things. I want to be up front so I don't surprise you. Is that OK with you?"

"Sure."

"All right. Before we get into it, I want to confirm that the outcome I'm looking for today is to have a free-flowing conversation so we can decide whether it's worth your time to schedule another call, or a visit, to see if we can help you going forward. Or maybe we're not the right fit, and we can recommend somebody else. Is that OK?"

"That sounds good, too."

(Transition to Marvin Gaye—What's going on?)

"Great. The first thing we typically do is let you, the customer, tell us what the situation is in your manufacturing facility and where you'd like to see it in the future. Talk to me about what that gap looks like, and I'll start to understand if we can help you or not."

"Here are some of our challenges: Our suppliers who shut down have a backlog of orders, and we've got new orders coming in. We still haven't found a way to get to our backlog yet. I'm starting to panic because I see so much revenue that's available, but I have to get my operations streamlined, and software might be the magic formula. What would you have that can help?"

"First of all, Dave, you're talking about things that are current. You're talking about stuff you're trying to process and turn around right now. I want to help you, but we're not going to be able to help you currently. There's nothing we can do in the next couple of weeks that will get your orders turned around or changed at all. Are you OK for us to keep talking?"

"If we could have something that's deployable in the next 30 to 60 days, that's more what I'm looking for."

"That's pushing it, but we can work toward that. We can keep talking, but I don't want to keep going and have you think I can change everything quickly. It's going to take 60 to 90 days if we really push, but let's keep going. There are a couple of things I need to know. You're talking about processing more orders, and you mentioned there's some chaos on the floor. Let's say we send our gurus up there, and they fix that for you. Roughly how much more money will you make a month because of that?"

"We've already been paid upfront on some of them, so I'm floating those orders because we haven't been able to service the new revenue coming in. I'm kind of far out on a limb, to speak financially, as a business owner. We have a 20 percent margin, which is the biggest we've ever seen. I'm happy to be there, and I want to get to that cash as fast as possible."

(When they lay out their numbers, the salesperson shows how their solution fits in.)

"Dave, I'll fast-forward a little bit. You're talking about $100,000 a month, roughly; let's just say a million dollars a year if you get this sorted out. That's a good problem to have. You've got a booming business. When I run into people like you, we typically provide you with an assessment of your situation. We can send one of our engineers up there for two days. They'll study your whole business with you, document it, then they'll come up with a proposal that says, for this much money and time, we'll get this problem solved for you. That costs $5,000 plus expenses. I don't know if it's worth that to you right now, and you might not even have time to deal with our guy, but that's how we would approach it. Does that make any sense to you?"

"What you just described makes perfect sense."

(The goal is not to do any proof or demos right now.)

"Great. If that works for you, let's talk about dates. Are you talking about next week or the week after? What works for you?"

(Once a date has been arranged, the salesperson can close the call.)

"Great. It's really simple. I'll introduce you to the guy who will be coming up there, I'll put the details and the fee in the email, and I'll book it."

That's the basic anatomy of a sales call. It's very personal. It's not a lot of paperwork. And it makes getting the order easy and clear.

You don't want to start doing demos too early in the process. It is often asked for by the prospect when they're not sure what else to do. They are conditioned to want to see a demo. Save the demo for later— once you better understand the problem and how you can solve it, and when you're sure the company is ready to make a move. By the time you do a demo, it will be the last step before they purchase.

I teach that the next step with an interested buyer has to have some commitment on their part to do something. It might be paying $5,000. It might be filling out a survey. It's something other than sending a couple of brochures and then calling every two weeks about the problem. You don't want to do that. You need a commitment.

Noobs screw up sales calls sometimes. This tends to happen in four main areas:

- Maybe they talked too much.
- Maybe they "topped" the prospect's story.
- Maybe they spent the bulk of the sales call explaining their company or product instead of understanding the customer.
- Maybe they didn't get around to discussing money, or how an order could get processed.

If they did any or all of these things, they would find themselves in Noob Purgatory. The prospect will not say yes or no. They will string the noob along forever with more questions, or with avoided calls and cancelled meetings. The noob may think the prospect is being a jackass, but the truth is, the prospect just hasn't gotten comfortable with the noob or the solution, and they're too nice to tell them to run along.

Follow your call script. Don't end up in Noobatory.

# DEALING WITH EQUALS

For my first few noob years in sales, I put the buyer on a pedestal. They had the money and the power, and I was cozying up to them hoping they would like me and "give" me some business. Noob mistake.

To graduate to sales pro, you need to think about things from the customer's perspective. Maybe this thing you're selling them for $100,000 might make them a million every year, so they ought to be kissing your ass. At the very least, things should start out on equal footing. Your attitude and confidence level have a lot to do with how you will get treated. Demand equal respect from the potential buyer in terms of when you are meeting, for how long, where, what you're going to cover, etc. Don't just "let them drive."

If you get pushback, consider it a sign of a bad fit. The prospects that argue with you about the agenda/rules for the meeting tend to be non-buyers. They like to watch, if you know what I mean.

Your mindset should be that you have something of great value and you only have so much time every day, so you want to make sure you are spending it with the right folks. You don't have to play every game. If someone does not want to play by your fair rules, get into a new game. Noobs chase and chase and chase rude prospects. Pros build a steady pipeline of good prospects and bring in the business as it makes sense for the clients.

## CUSTOMER RELATIONSHIP MANAGEMENT FOR NOOBS

One of the most common tools that salespeople have to use, especially when they're not setting up an instantaneous transaction, is customer relationship management software, or CRM. If you're gathering a cus- tomer's information, even if it's a B2C relationship, there's probably a customer rewards number and account. Knowing how to handle your customer information, and the technology involved, makes a difference.

Sometimes noobs are intimidated by the idea of using technology or a database, especially if they don't understand why their employer wants to use databases in the first place. Even if it's a little inconvenient to put in people's information, it's so important to have that personal network. Your network compounds over time.

It's easier to do now than it used to be. I lost touch with certain people I was friends with in college, but it would've made really good sense for me to have purposely stayed connected to them to some degree, even if it was once a year to ask what they were up to. Some people with some common interests use a platform like HubSpot or Cloze. There are multiple free platforms that offer this network you'll want to develop over time and share ideas with. HubSpot has a great free version that I have used. If you just start adding the business people you run across, folks you think are worth staying in touch with once a year, you will be amazed at the power you will have developed in 10 years.

Salespeople throw so many of these opportunities away. Think about the stories of people who went to Harvard Business School, which is the greatest business networking place you could go to. Everyone who goes there has a plan to be a big-time business person. I've got a few friends who went there, and they're able to get these mega-successful people on the phone because they knew them in business school.

Even if you don't know someone that extreme yet, I recommend that you start with your own network and build it up over time. You don't know where your network will be in five to 10 years. It can help you to flesh out ideas. It can help you to get your next opportunity. You could let it be known that you're looking to buy a business. That's one side of networking.

When you start a job with a company, I would be amazed if you don't have to log on for your territory every morning. The most common CRM is Salesforce.com. When you're working for somebody's company, they're going to tell you what to use and how to use it. They're going to set the tone for how much time they want you to spend filling out forms in the system. How accurate do you want to keep things? Some companies won't care as long as you sell. Others will be more rigid and say that you must keep an appointment because you filled it out in your forms. Some places expect that every time you talk to someone, you update the records.

It makes my heart race a little when I think about how much time is wasted on these reports. Your personal network is what you want to tend to first to help you with all kinds of things in life. And you help them, too. These are not random people but relationships you nurture on purpose. Then, when you get to your company, they're going to lead the way in terms of what you're using and how they want you to use it. Do not get carried away with thinking that you're doing a good sales job because you're filling out records. Fill it out, but don't make that your sole focus. Remember, you want to get in the customer's shoes—not the CRM manager's!

CRMs can seriously cut into people's time. You could spend your entire day inside the system. But it's a big-time saver if you have the next day roughly mapped out. At the end of the day, plan out the next day: the five prospecting calls that you're going to make, the 10 people you're going to try to schedule appointments with, and the three conference calls you have scheduled. That way, you can see what your day looks like. You'll be happy to share that with your manager. After you finish a phone call, quickly enter it into the system and then go to the next thing.

It's normal to think you can make all these calls and then do the notes at the end of the day, but that's a bad idea because you'll forget some details. Do it as you go. Noobs wait till later, pros do it now. Prep for a call—have the call—then do call follow-up. Repeat.

Remember: First, plan your day so that it aligns with your goals. Second, update the CRM as you go, but don't confuse looking at your computer screen with selling!

One of our alums is Scott Millwood. He agrees with me about how stupid it is to have reps spending too much screen time versus customer time. I must say, when we hired Scott, he was already a sales pro and he really helped all of us move up the food chain of selling to larger enterprises. Not surprisingly, he has continued to be successful with several companies that he started since our time together at Datastream. His current company, Yesflow, is making it easier for sales reps to get and give information to the CRM. He doesn't believe it's a good idea to have reps sitting in their office typing all day. The Yesflow technology can work through your iPhone or Alexa, making the communication back and forth with the CRM verbally a lot easier for reps to keep up while on the go.

Customer data is the most valuable aspect of an employer's business. Even above the product you sell, your customer list (especially if it's in the tens of thousands) can sell for two or three dollars per person or more, depending on the type of industry. The more information you have on your customers, the more valuable the business is.

Think of it this way: The more information your employer has on your customers, the easier it's going to be to continue engaging them and selling to them. The average customer lifetime value increases when you engage with them, meaning they spend more money because you're able to keep in touch with them and send birthday cards and those sorts of special things. The bigger the network, the longer you are going to have a job and the more valuable you're going to be.

While working in your entry-level sales job, get into the habit now of getting as much information about customers as possible. When it comes time for you to do enterprise sales and manage the accounts, you'll know what to listen for, what to look for, and what to put in your CRM. Even if you're working in B2C sales right now, being aware of all the information you would want to know about your customers sets you up for success down the line.

You've got your friends and family, you've got your best friends, and you've got this broader network that you want to stay in touch with. Maybe that's 50 people. Beyond that, even if you're selling phones for Apple, connect on LinkedIn with everyone you meet that's interesting so you'll always have access to them. It's like a gold mine.

As noobs, you don't know it yet, but the noobs you're meeting are going to be CEOs in 20 or 25 years. They might be running the local hospital or be the VP of a company you need to connect with. If you make an effort to get to know those people just a little bit, the rewards could be amazing. I know some people who are just phenomenal at this. They stay in touch with me, and I feel like I'm their best friend. I'm sure they've got a great system where they're staying in touch with people who might be helpful to them.

A smart tactic I've seen salespeople do is make their own personal spreadsheet of contacts who might be able to introduce them to customers. We call these referral partners. People you have a great rapport with and want to stay connected to because they work at the chamber of commerce, for example. Basically, leads that lead to leads. These are people who could connect you to the people you want to know, who you can reach out to and ask for a favor. I knew someone who did this because he recognized the value in it. When he returned to the area a couple of years ago, he reached out to some of his contacts to tell them he was back in town, and they offered him a job even after two years of not seeing him.

Get your own CRM that lists the names of the people you're interested in staying in touch with and what you know about them. What common interests do you have?

My son, Jack Sterling, sells a variety of telecom and cloud-related products to area businesses. His best lead sources are people who run IT companies. They're providing services to the same kinds of businesses he's selling telecom to, and they're very happy to have a source to give leads to because they don't want to mess with that aspect. They don't do telecom.

The key is to select your network carefully and know that it's a long-term deal. Don't meet with someone and immediately ask for some leads just because they're with the chamber of commerce. Nobody in their right mind would do that. They would want to hear more about your business and how it's going. Then, after meeting with them a second or third time, they might say there's someone you should talk to. Think long-term and strategic, and remember that more is less. Stay focused on the very best partners for you.

Choose your core group of influencers and then take it slow. Start a drip campaign with them. Meet up and go for a walk. Ask if you can buy them a coffee. Tell them you want to show them your new office. Just don't do too much. Get a feel for whether there's something there. If not, find another one. If there is, work it slowly and help them be a good vendor for whoever it is they have access to.

Keep in mind that although not everyone will necessarily offer a complementary service, they may still reach the same type of customers. Through my Foxfire business, we get leads from our website from interested people. When you start a campaign, the odds are pretty low for closing a random lead that comes in from anywhere. But we also have partners. We have relationships with resellers around the country who, for many years, built their business by calling on warehouses and selling them all the stuff a warehouse needs. When one of their customers needs software, they recommend us, and it's a 50 percent chance of a win. We spend our time working with those people, making sure they're comfortable with what we're doing when they run across these opportunities in their own customer base. It works great for us and is much better than a lead conversion. And not just a little better: working a lead from a trusted partner is 10 times more likely to become a sale!

I wish all sales were as easy as receiving an emphatic "yes" to the question, "Would you like to buy this new iPhone?" But you'll get push-back at least half the time.

How can you push back so the prospect falls right into the sale? That's up next.

# CHAPTER 6

# NEGOTIATION AND OBJECTION HANDLING MADE EASY

S weaty palms. Hot tempers. Big drama. That's what most sales noobs expect negotiation to be like.

But that's Hollywood. If you're doing it that way, you're probably doing it wrong. Negotiation should be a back-and-forth conversation where you try to find a price and terms that work for everyone's mutual benefit. Is this deal worth it to the customer and to you, the salesperson? If you can help each other answer that question in the affir- mative, you've got yourself a sale.

This chapter is all about helping you get there. I'm happy to acknowl- edge that our friend Bill Garcia at Tableforce.com trained me and our entire 100-person global salesforce on negotiations. Bill helped us all understand and get comfortable with negotiating fairly for our company, our customers, and ourselves.

As you've come to expect from this book, you're about to learn the fundamentals of how *not* to negotiate and objection handle. Let's dig in.

# Seven Negotiation and Objection Mistakes Noobs Make (That You Don't Have To)

## Assuming the Customer Is Always Right

First things first, get it out of your head that the customer is always right.

I meet people who still believe that this is the case, including some of my clients. That statement is head trash, but it's in the common belief system because someone said it a long time ago and it keeps get- ting repeated.

Most of us have seen that the 80/20 rule, Pareto's principle, is almost always in effect with your customers. You have 20 percent of your cus- tomers taking up 80 percent of your time in terms of customer service. It's the same for any other type of issue. If you're looking at your busi- ness by the numbers, those customers are costing you more money than the others. They're not as profitable and they're taking away your energy. When you own a business, you find that out pretty quickly. The other thing you learn is that if you treat all your customers the same, you're being quite foolish.

One day you might sell to a branch of Exxon, where a refinery would buy your software. Next week you might sell it to Mama Jo's Moon Pie factory. They both go in the system—as customer number one and customer number two—and you'll call them twice a year to see how they're doing.

Employees are very important to the company. If your customers are breaking the agreement with how to treat each other in a business set- ting, and running your employees into the ground, then you don't need them. Take care of your people.

The other reason you might say a customer is *not* always right is if they don't pay you, are slow to pay, or argue about the bill every month. A small percentage of people will be like that. In my experience, you should not think the customer is always right. Let them have a relationship with another business and become someone else's headache. You want to focus on the people who are following the agreement and paying when they're supposed to.

There are plenty of reasons why the customer could be wrong. It's a mistake to think you should try to please everyone. Instead, focus the bulk of your attention on the 20 percent of your customers bringing in 80 percent of the revenue. You can deal with problem customers in the time left over. Or, better yet, let them find a new vendor.

Signs of customers you don't want: They're slow to pay, complain a lot, are rude, take a lot of customer service time, and are overly demanding. When you see these traits, it's time to move on!

## FAILING TO WIDEN THE GAP (CREATING YOUR NEGOTIATING LEVERAGE)

How do you widen the gap from the buyer's perspective so you're more likely to get a "yes" instead of a "maybe later" or a "no"?

Where is the prospect now, and where do they want to be? Is there a way to ethically widen that gap? Not to make their life harder, but to put in perspective how valuable you are as a gap closer. Find a way to increase that sense of urgency for your prospect so that you get to the yes sooner.

Most salespeople don't follow this process. Noobs are more likely to push how good their product is without understanding the real problem that needs to be solved. The more you dig and understand the problem, what issues it is causing, how long it has been going on, and what will happen to your buyer if they don't get it fixed, the easier your leverage becomes. Yes, some of these questions require lots of time and patience to pull the information out. Also, it requires great tact, and a certain empathy and smooth factor, to get some of the personal information. Remember, you can write the questions down in the correct order and practice beforehand. Even experienced pros use lists—I still do.

So, how does this relate to negotiating as a noob? If you go into the call and start yapping about how great you are, or your company is, or the product, or how many reps you have, you lose your prospects. They couldn't care less.

Here is a summary secret. If you just understand this, you'll blow through noob and go right to pro!

- Prospects only care about themselves (no matter how cool you are, and even if they act interested).
- Prospects won't come out and tell you what the real problem is. You must dig it out. (Ever fibbed to your doctor about a problem?)
- Once you ID the real problem, they'll be so happy with you you'll get the first shot at solving it. (Finally, somebody gets them.)

Understand and follow these truths to move past being a noob.

In other words, it's about them, not you. It's about the problem they have, not your product.

The best time to win a negotiation is before it even starts. Find the prospects that you can help the most, help them understand why you're their best shot, and you'll have all the leverage you need to get a   fair price.

Beyond that, the next best negotiating tip for a noob is to use the "higher authority" method. Until you have the training—and permission from the company—to negotiate price, focus on finding the great opportunities, getting the sales pros out there that have the right tools, and when the prospect wants to negotiate, just say you have to take any questions about price or terms back to HQ. Collaborate with your management for the best reply, and always get something in return if you are going to give something! Your management should be able to help with that. In the meantime, you're proving to them that getting you trained in negotiations is a must.

# ASSUMING THEY CAN'T AFFORD IT

Noobs often assume that the high-ticket product or service they offer is too expensive and no prospect can afford it. This can happen when they're selling for a big company at their first sales gig and have never seen so many zeroes on a price tag. Noobs confuse how they relate to money on their own level of wealth with how the customer relates to money.

A million dollars is a lot of money to most people, especially a noob just starting out, but it's pocket change to someone at Exxon who is responsible for spending hundreds of millions of dollars a year in their budget. That is one of the reasons noobs need to study accounting, at least the basics, so they can understand how money works in the businesses they are calling. Otherwise, it will be a mystery how their product might affect the customer's profit and loss statement, balance sheet, cash flow, stock price, etc.

Assuming the prospect can't afford your product is a losing game that stops you from trying your best to close the deal. That head trash can come up as a problem for salespeople in multiple ways. There are a couple of layers to it.

We begin with the relative value of money. When you're starting out as a new salesperson, normally you don't have a lot of money. The idea of spending $1,000 on a product is a big deal when even $100 to go out to dinner is impossible on your starting budget. That's a portion of your rent! Then, you pick up the phone and talk with multimillion-dollar business owners, and there's the potential for million-dollar deals. You need to get out of your own financial perspective and think like your prospect. Pretend you are them instead, and do the math on this deal from their perspective.

Our sales team at Datastream started out selling $5,000 deals. Five years later, that became $50,000 deals. Five years after that, $100,000 deals, followed by $1 million deals. After 20 years, million-dollar deals became the norm, and now the company has sold one enterprise deal for $100 million! That's as much as we used to sell in our best years. It was the same company with the same people, just older and more experienced selling larger deals and dealing with senior-level executives.

That's a big part of what you see in a 50-year-old killer salesperson who's doing big deals and is comfortable at the CEO and CFO level. They've hung in there long enough to learn the secrets. But all reps started as noobs. You need to recognize your limiting thoughts so you aren't in awe of the big numbers or high-level people. Then you will move up the food chain faster to bigger deals.

It's normal to be timid around money or numbers. To overcome this, go back to what we talked about earlier. Don't even think about the price of the system until you figure out its value to the prospect's situation. If you say the value is going to be roughly 1 percent of the value of their physical assets, and their physical assets are $100 billion, 1 percent of that is $1 billion. Your product is worth a billion dollars to them. Price your product less than that, and you're cutting them a killer deal. You're doing them an immense favor by selling them what seems like a high-ticket product from your perspective.

I had a salesperson, once he got a bit older, who went to Georgia Pacific before they sold and said he wanted to upgrade their system. He checked the contract, did the math, and calculated that they had 467 facilities. So, the deal was worth $13 million at the price they had agreed to per site. They agreed with him. He got 8 percent—a $1 million commission—all because he started by looking at the value to the prospect. He backed it down to what the number looked like for Georgia Pacific.

A lot of salespeople, especially when they're young, leave a ton of money on the table because they're nervous. They want to get the sale quickly. They want to do the person a favor. There are lots of reasons. Before you head into every deal, do the math on what this could be worth to your prospect.

Focus on your prospect's problem first before you think about your product.

Focus on the financial value your product could bring to the table.

Then compare that value to the price you're charging.

You'll probably be surprised you're charging so little for the generated value.

# FROM NOOB TO PRO: ADVANCED NEGOTIATION AND OBJECTION HANDLING

By now, you know how to handle objections with ease and lead prospects right to the sale. The art and science of selling is only a share of the sales career prize. In the same way that you have to know how to sell your product or service to customers, you need to be able to sell yourself to employers. That's less about talking a big game and more about playing it. Let's see what I mean.

# CHAPTER 7

# BETTER JOB, HIGHER PAY, MORE PROMOTIONS

"**O**nce a noob, always a noob."

Wrong. Two or three years into your sales job, you'll be well beyond noob. You'll know your way around prospects' businesses to the point you can dismiss objections before they come up and run calculations on the fly that justify your price. It will seem easy.

If only everything about sales were so easy. Running parallel to your selling skill is career building. Junior sales reps don't want to stay sales reps. You may want to move companies, get promoted, be a manager, or start a business—there are endless options once you can sell like a champ.

In this chapter, I'll show you how to grow your career. I'll teach you what not to do and how to avoid mistakes. Read on, and don't noob yourself!

# Ten Career Growth Mistakes Noobs Make (That You Don't Have To)
## Skipping Sales Training

From the beginning, many noobs think that training is stupid. That it's a waste of time because they could be on the phone selling instead. Then they imagine they don't need to listen to their manager or to whoever is training them. They know what they're doing or will figure it out as they go.

In the same way, noobs resist the new language that comes with the new job, including new vocabulary around the business they are selling for. Companies have unique names and nicknames for things that the noob needs to embrace and not question for being different. The same goes for your sales training. You will be getting all sorts of new buzzwords around things like "sales cycles," VITO letters, and "closing."

My advice: Just go with it. You are now living among people who speak a slightly different language. The quicker you adopt it, the quicker you can turn pro. Being resistant to training simply shows your head is not in the game. Every million-dollar salesperson credits ongoing training as one of the main drivers of their success.

In the beginning, you should tweak out on learning everything about your customers, your product and sales skills, and best practices to be successful. Once you pass the noob stage, let's say at a year, you can back off some training to at least a weekly schedule on anything you want to keep getting better at.

I'm in my 50s and still do weekly training on finance, entrepreneurism, music lessons, and yes, sales. And I literally wrote the book on selling, which you hold in your hands! If I'm still learning, you should be, too. If you're serious about making sales work for you, you must commit to training. It can be 15 minutes of free YouTube instruction, a high-paid one-on-one coach, and everything in between. The main thing is to commit to something on the calendar at least weekly.

It might sound counterproductive, but you want to spend more time learning about what you're doing than actually doing it. Too many sales jobs begin with almost no learning. You spend all your time on the phone. Before we enforced our training program, people were working really hard but making the same mistakes over and over again, using the wrong words or talking too much.

When I was first starting out, I was always too busy to seek out training. When I finally did, and I learned negotiation training and proper hiring training, it was like a huge lever that brought me back to the company. But then I'd forget how great the training results were, and I would be too busy to do it again. You can make it in sales and in business without much training, it's just going to be harder and take more time.

If you don't train early, you're going to make the same mistakes over and over again. Yes, people can make the exact same mistakes at the five-year, ten-year, and 15-year marks because they haven't trained. Mentor groups, peer groups, or a good breakfast club can be beneficial.

Realize that training and self-improvement must be constant if you want to become your best.

## ENDING YOUR EDUCATION AFTER SCHOOL

When I was in school, one of my pieces of head trash was that I "didn't need an MBA." I thought it was a waste of time and that I'd be better off in a company learning something. I've overcome not having a business degree, but it would have been much easier if I'd understood the basics of a profit and loss (P&L) statement and a balance sheet, how businesses generally raise money, and other accounting vocabulary.

My advice: Learn basic accounting—it is the language of business.

Acquiring some form of education to get ready for your craft, or in addition to being an apprentice, is wonderful. The founder of UGG® boots, Brian Smith, started his business after moving from Australia to California. He sold it for something like $4 billion and was able to pocket most of it because it was a private company. He and his wife were the two co-founders of an international empire. After I heard him speak, I asked him what he thought businesspeople might be missing in terms of their skill set. He singled out accounting. Either you need to become obsessed with accounting, or you need to find a partner who is.

I came to this later in life, but this is something I can pass on. There's still some head trash in people who want to be entrepreneurs. They say, "Screw the accounting people. They're just bookkeepers and numbers crunchers." Wrong. You'd better get 80 percent knowledge on that topic if you want to succeed. And you can do it online these days, without spending two years in business school!

Learning about accounting means learning to understand the profit and loss statement, the balance sheet, the cash flow statement, the underlying importance of the cash flow statement, and how to collect money.

You might wonder why a salesperson needs to do any of that at the beginning of their career. In sales, one of the things I completely missed for a whole decade was tying my job to a company's ROI each year and then applying that to their balance sheet. That's the Holy Grail, and it's easy to do once you understand it.

If you can understand that flow, you can go to the prospect and say, "We did some homework. I know you did a million dollars in earnings (or retained earnings) per share last year. The math we did with a third-party consultant shows if you replace all your valves with us, you can write that stuff off. There's going to be no hit to your balance sheet over 10 years, and we'll be able to turn that into $1.4 million. If your stock multiplier holds, you'll go from $28 to $62 a share in one year. According to your annual report, your family trust owns a million shares, so all else being equal, if we go forward, your family trust value will increase by $16 million in two years. What do you think we should do now?"

Being able to offer that type of precise information is exactly the reason you want to understand accounting as a salesperson. The first time it happened to me, some guy was trying to sell me a new CRM when we already had a patchwork CRM that worked fine. I questioned why we would buy it because, to me, it was a new expense, and we'd all have to learn a new system. He calmly said, "We found most people who go from the kind of system you have to our system see sales go up about 10 percent."

I said, "I'll take it."

Accounting isn't just about numbers. It's a persuasion tool.

## MIXING UP EDUCATION AND EXPERIENCE

Twenty years ago, it was pretty well believed that if you knew someone who hadn't graduated from college, they had blown it.

Then came Gates, Zuckerberg, and Jobs. They are the first ones I can remember who were obvious phenoms who didn't finish college. I think the coronavirus has turned education on its ear. If you want to spend $30,000 a semester for video lectures on computer science, then Gates ought to be teaching the class. It should be the absolute best person.

I went to a music camp for a week in the summer of 2018. It was mostly high school kids but also some adults. One of the guys got up on stage and asked the high schoolers, "Are any of you planning to study music in college?" They all raised their hands. He said, "Have you ever thought about hiring the best teacher and taking a lesson every day and practicing? Get a lesson, practice, get a lesson, practice. Imagine if you did that for four years. How good would you be instead of going to college, studying music theory, and sitting in classes, most of which are going to be boring and won't help you?"

College used to be a rite of passage (or a ticket of admission) to get into various levels of the dance. Now it's more about the skill sets and knowledge you bring to the table.

It doesn't matter where you got them. You might not have gone to college, but you spent three years working for a great sales company. Compare that experience to someone who went to Brown University and majored in poetry and earned a degree. If you're matching these two people up for sales, it's not a fair fight, not even close.

It won't hurt you to go to Brown and major in poetry, but if you are in that position and want to go into sales, get some experience while you are in school. Your poetry degree won't impress hiring sales managers, but your experience will.

# STAYING IN YOUR LANE

If sales is your career, the only credentials that matter are things you have learned or experienced that can help you sell. In sales, you are judged by your number. What you sell on average every month, every quarter, every year.

Sales is a great leveler of degree versus skill because it comes out in the numbers, between knowing what you're doing, having guts, and working hard. I have never seen a sales rep do all of the "right things"—like the "dos" we talk about in this book—and fail to do well. It is inevitable to succeed when you do it all right, but it may take more time than you like. As with most things in life, it takes time to reap the benefits of hard work, practice, and good training. But it will pay off.

I have also seen reps skip steps in the process. Some of them actually do okay for a while. Sometimes they get lucky, or take a shortcut that looks good in the moment. This is never a good long-term plan because you didn't get where you did with a consistent or sustainable method. You jumped, and you may not be able to jump like that again. Keep your growth consistent and your accomplishments repeatable. That means you keep training.

There will always be exceptions, but in a perfect world, a great salesperson or business owner understands what's happening at the field level. In a perfect world, they've been out there, they've used the product, and they're in the field doing it. They're not just learning about it at a seminar. They can say they've been in 24 other businesses like yours in the last two years and have helped achieve cost savings results between 10 percent and 14 percent. Just like a doctor can say he can take care of your hand because he's done 224 hand operations like yours in the last three years. Experience is extremely valuable when you are calling on any buyer, but especially business owners.

Imagine you own a business, and a sales rep wants to make a call on you. Why would you bother seeing her in the first place? Only if you thought she could help you save—or make —more

———

126

money. I love hearing from these kinds of salespeople. The ones who try to sell me something without much regard for my benefit (i.e., the sale is clearly the goal here, not me) won't get any of my time. You can hear the approach in their voice. Is this sale going to be about them or me, the customer?

It's also important to get past the veneer or filter most people have when they start a conversation with somebody new. They change into a different person by adopting a more formal tone when they address a new prospect. Your tone is ultra-important. And the funny thing is, we make it hard on ourselves because most noobs try to sound crisp and businesslike. Just be yourself. Soften the tone. Chill.

I've had thousands of conversations myself, and listened to thousands of recorded sales calls. Hundreds of times I've heard the prospect tense up because the salesperson sounded too "official." I've never heard a prospect be offended by a rep sounding more casual. Make it easy on yourself and just talk normal, like you're calling your cousin to help him out.

Now, casual is fine. But speaking good English is still important. If you don't have a handle on grammar, say as few words as possible and get some training and practice as soon as you can. A prospect won't explicitly say they didn't go with you because you have bad grammar, but they will pass you over. Rightly or wrongly, they will use this against you.

The talent stack idea comes from *How to Fail at Almost Everything and Still Win Big* by Scott Adams.[6] That book made a lot of sense to me. After reading it, I recognized that out of the hundreds of reps I've worked with, the ones at the very top of the sales pyramid had developed talent stacks that included more than just sales mastery. A few had taken time to serve the country as officers in the Army and developed incredible leadership skills that carried over to big company sales leadership roles. Several had gotten MBAs, Toastmasters Certification, Sandler Sales Training, Tableforce.com Negotiation Training, and Solution Selling Training. And in some cases, degrees or certifications in areas more closely aligned to the vertical they serve.

---

6    Scott Adams, How to Fail at Almost Everything and Still Win Big: Kind of the Story of My Life (New York: Portfolio / Penguin, 2013)

Some of the reps kept adding to that skill stack and absolutely crushed it.

Growing your talent stack is a patient person's game. I highly recommend it if you want to move up the food chain.

As you're learning different things (i.e., skill stacking), the skills you acquire should be related to your field. For example, if you worked for a music store chain as a buyer, you could either:

a) Show up for work every day, do a good job, gain knowledge with time, and hopefully move up.

b) Show up for work every day, but also take up an instrument to better understand your buyer, get your MBA online, take a course in franchising, take a course in public speaking, take a course in web selling and internet marketing, start a LinkedIn group of music store sellers, etc.

You get the idea. The option "b" person will move up 10 times faster than option "a." If option "b" also started some weird talent like beekeeping, that would be fine, but it doesn't really add to the plan. In other words, I encourage you to stack a bunch of skills toward your specific goal, don't just do a bunch of random stuff, and hope that future employers will look for a VP of sales with beekeeping experience.

Spending time on the simple skills I've listed below is great for talent stacking and will improve your sales. None of these have to be mastered at the expert level to reap the benefits. You don't need to be the very best, just proficient.

- Refine your manners and etiquette.
- Learn how to dress appropriately for different groups of people.
- Spend time on your health. People are much more likely to buy from someone who's impressively healthy and able to work.
- Take finance training, whether it's an online MBA or a mini MBA, or something where you understand the language of business.

The reason we get away with not being better is that most salespeople are not talent-stacked like they should be. If you are competing with a bad noob and you are an ok noob, you'll win. But that does not make you a pro. A pro is the option "b" person above after about five years of talent stacking. Plan for the long game.

Remember that the business owner is only thinking about how much your product will cost them versus how much money they will make from it. They're wondering how they'll pay for it and also about the terms, the ROI, the guarantee, and the return policy. It's just numbers to them. They couldn't care less about how the software is made or what the machinery looks like. Your company cares about features and technology, close attempts, tricky ways to get a deal done, specials, and incentives, but your prospect does not. That's what most noobs don't get. You can mention a few things your customer doesn't care about and still carry the sale, sure. But this book is about going pro, so make sure you speak in the customer's language and keep the discussion about them—not you!

I used to believe (my head trash) that accounting was for weenies. That we could just hire an accountant if we needed one. I believed this until I read that Warren Buffett suggested everyone study accounting because so many business leaders don't understand it. It's the lan- guage of business. He said entering the business world and not knowing accounting would be like moving to Germany and not learning how to speak German. You need to understand accounting to be as effective as you can. In today's world, I would also learn the history of computer science and how to do basic coding and design. If all that sounds intimi- dating, you can learn the essentials of any field in a few weeks at Udemy or Khan Academy.

Your selling training is also very important. There are more than enough places with consistent selling methodologies and ways to get trained, from Stephen Covey to Zig Ziglar, Sandler, and beyond. I'm a big fan of Sandler Training because I love the format of learning something new every week and reinforcing it forever.

When you're in sales, you're closest to the money. It's the most rewarding because it's a show-me-the-money job. But there are so many other functions of business that you must understand. You need to be able to see every deal from the perspective of the decision-makers, the people you're selling to that are writing a check to buy your product or service. If this is a B2B sale, noobs should understand that the biggest money is in enterprise sales. You can become a millionaire in one year with a few nice enterprise deals, but most people probably aren't going to start there.

Instead, noobs will typically be given the smaller accounts and will work their way up to the larger opportunities. It's really important that they build that talent stack as early as possible. From the B2B sales viewpoint, they must understand that the business owner lives in a world of accounting, profit and loss, equity-to-debt ratio, and marketing. The more you understand about your business clients, the more you'll understand how useful your product or service will be to them. Do that, and you'll have more opportunities to sell them on the value of your product or service.

A salesperson needs to be able to think like their business- owner client or as a high-level decision-maker at their client's company. A pro trick is to ask, "How can I use my network to bring a new customer to my prospect?" If you can figure this out, your relationship with the prospect will go up a few notches, and your chance of making big sales will increase dramatically. You get into a different game when you bring them customers. Now, when they see you coming, they won't see a cost—they'll see revenue!

Yet another easy pro trick is to hang around places your potential customers hang out. In a perfect world, what you sell will be something you love and use. Short of that, you can schedule time, like a few hours a week, to just hang out with your customers in the environment where they're using your product. Or maybe you attend a convention where your customers find out about new products in the industry, including yours. Find out what they love about it, hate about it, etc. See what marketing gets them most excited. You will get an invaluable education that will put you in a different position than the noobs. And oddly enough, those customers will likely become bigger customers and more willing reps because you are spending time with them. You become one of them, and they'll want to support one of their own. At a minimum, I would shoot for a learning visit once a week, as close as possible to your office.

For example, if you're in the trucking business, your process could be as simple as hanging out with the truckers every Friday afternoon, walking around the warehouse and finding out what's happening. You'll start to learn what's really going on in the business. If you have the life experience, try to connect it to what you're selling. If you're sell- ing a product specifically for consumers, you don't need to understand accounting and marketing and everything else, but it will help you build rapport or share insights into your prospect's situation. You need to know the real-world use and benefits of all the features and functions of the product or service you're selling.

One good question to get used to asking your sales manager or even yourself is, "What does integrating our product/service look like for consumers?"

## STAYING AWAY FROM ENTERPRISE SALES

I started at the lower end of sales doing mostly over-the-phone and lower-cost transactional-type selling. I crawled and scratched my way up the hill. Most experienced salespeople did it this way. Almost none of us started big. We were all noobs, too.

Eventually, we got bigger and bigger. By the time we'd figured it out, we were doing million-dollar deals. They actually weren't that dif-ficult once we learned how to do them. If you've got a company with 75 locations around the world and your product is already carried in six of them, when you have the conversation with the CFO about expanding, it's either a "yes" or a "no." If they want to standardize your product, you negotiate a global deal. There's no in-between.

Noobs are often intimidated by that potential, but you should start thinking like that. A quick conversation with a CFO won't hurt a thing. You just want to meet them and get it on their radar that rolling up all sites to one standard (yours) is a possibility. If you want reinforcement, ask your owner or manager to come with you to meet the CFO, or even the CEO. These folks like meeting each other, so use that to get meetings.

I recommend that salespeople, even when they're new, at least think about arranging these bigger deals with broader companies. If you're dealing with the Michelin facility in North Charleston, think about Michelin as a company. Where are they headquartered? How many facilities are there? Who is the CFO? If you were going to do a deal with the whole company, who would you need to talk to? This can scare a 22-year-old salesperson, but it shouldn't. Why don't you ask the owner of your company what they think about it?

Think about the bigger perspective from the start. Think of it like a puzzle—one that takes a few years to put together. Go ahead and start assembling the pieces now. By the time that multimillion-dollar global deal is ready, you'll have grown enough to handle it.

## PUSHING YOURSELF TOO FAR TOO SOON

People get nervous about having a gap year on their résumé.

They're told (head trash) that this is bad. Résumé expectations are different now because there are so many independent contractors. But people still worry about that gap year. They expect that dreaded interview question: "What did you do that year?" If you sat around watching Netflix and smoking weed, you should probably be a little nervous. If you went to a surf camp in Brazil and tried to write a novel, that's a win as far as I'm concerned. I want people who are risk-takers and who are interesting. But people get weird about trying to do everything within the bounds of society, and they worry about something small like a gap year disqualifying them.

The same flawed thinking applies to college. College is being flipped on its head right now. But many people still think they must go to school and graduate in four years. I believe that one of the most important things you can do is get out, see the world, and get some work experience, even if it takes you five years or more to finish college. And that's if you even decide to pursue college, as we discussed previously. If you're traveling around and supporting yourself, it makes you a much more valuable person when it comes time to interview.

Previously, when we talked about people who were at the beginning of their careers, we discussed the idea that hobbies and travel can be a waste of time. If your objective is to be as successful as possible, you're going to have to make some sacrifices. There are going to be some things you don't get to do because they're distractions. In that context, you should travel before you engage in the sales profession. At the same time, if you're on the clock and working down the path, you'll add to your effectiveness if you already know what you want to go into. If that's the case, try to incorporate that into your travel. Then your traveling time will become a valuable learning experience.

If you wanted to go into engineering and arranged a yearlong trip around the world to visit CERN, the largest particle physics laboratory in the world, and other great engineering-focused places, this would be a valuable use of time that you can apply when you go to work for an engineering company. Then, when they ask what you did that year, and you reply that you wrote an engineering blog while visiting the great engineering masterpieces of the world, you will be a hot commodity. Moreover, you'll have a base of knowledge in your field that few others will.

Most colleges offer online options now anyway. Why not zip around the world? Worried about travel restrictions? Don't let that head trash stop you. First, all travel is not restricted, just some specific areas, and you will be able to find ways to get where you want to go. Second, since fewer folks are traveling, you will be welcomed more warmly wherever you go. All pros know that showing up has huge power.

Reach out to leaders in your desired industry and make a connection. Set up a meeting while you're in the area. Example: "I am thinking about coming to Singapore and would like to meet you. Would that be OK?" Or: "I'm in Singapore visiting all the best engineering feats in the world. Could I meet you while I am here and ask a few questions?"

Don't be afraid to take the time you need to begin your career on the best foot.

# LOOKING FOR PERFECT

Too many noobs get discouraged when everything in their life doesn't run perfectly. They get stuck on the idea that they're working for the wrong company. Or they decide their manager is not good. Or they believe all the training time their company encourages is a waste of time.

I've heard it all, believe me. But the winners don't get bogged down with discouraging self-talk. They find a way to win.

Determine what formula you can use to get what you want. Your situation is never going to be perfect. And there's more than one version of good enough, so you've got choices. Go ahead and work toward your goals where you are while you look for a better opportunity.

# WHINING

Don't complain or whine, no matter what is happening. No one wants to hear it.

The sales industry does not treat whiners well. We deal in problems. Big problems create big opportunities. It's important to have a mentality in sales that you're not going to whine or complain about not being lucky, or anything else that sounds negative. Your job is to take problems and find solutions. Whining means you haven't taken your job to heart.

Remember, bad things are going to happen. Let's say, for example, that you're a young salesperson and you've got your biggest account. You've done a really good job—you've researched it, you have a good relationship with the buyer, and you can really provide them with value. Then the company goes out of business. Your first response might be to complain that it should have happened to someone else, or your numbers should be changed, or it's not fair.

Complaining does nothing.

Most people fall into the trap of thinking everything is bad, and somehow, they got screwed. But there's another way to look at this situation. Instead, ask yourself how you got that account in the first place. By providing value through a relationship, right? So, think about the transition that the employees at the company are going through. Vow to do everything you can to help your contacts find new opportunities with your other customers. The money and the numbers will work themselves out.

Be helpful in this situation. Expect something good to come of it. You know that in other situations when companies have gone under or changed, people have reinvented themselves. Maybe this temporary setback will bring a bigger deal down the line. Maybe you'll eventually have 10 larger customers who scatter from this one company. If you don't have that secondary attitude, then you won't have a chance for those things to happen. You've ruled it out by being negative.

If you whine and complain and never call those people—and stay stuck in a bad-luck mentality—then you've ruled out the possibility of anything good happening. If you have a positive attitude in a bad situation, some good things will come from it. Relationships will continue. Your contacts will start working in other places, in new lines of business. They'll never forget that you helped them when the chips were down or that you helped them just to help—not for a commission.

Gratitude is huge down the line. Big business deals get decided on relationships.

If you're the whiner, then typically, you're not going to get picked as a keeper. Your company might say they had to cut down to eight people, no hard feelings. You're the last person in and the first one out. That's how things will go. They won't tell you they don't want you around because you're a whiny baby.

I've seen people handle getting laid off beautifully. We had a guy named David Laura, who is from Mexico and went to The Citadel playing tennis on a scholarship. I hired him out of school, as I did many of those cadets. David was really excited to be working for this great technology company like so many others he knew that had graduated before him. In between making him an offer and his start date, we sold the company. During that time, we were required to put all offers on hold.

I had to tell him that I didn't have a job for him. I couldn't have felt worse. I told him I'd do whatever I could to help him, but it wasn't our company anymore. He responded, "No problem. Don't worry about it. It'll work out. I know you're doing the best you can." He was a college senior looking for his first job, and he'd just lost a great opportunity, yet he had a great attitude at that moment. I had nothing to offer other than to be his friend.

In the end, I didn't get him another job. He had problems with his visa and had to go back to Mexico. Another setback. But his attitude remained strong that good things would work out.

Indeed, they did. Today, David runs the Latin American regions for a large software company and has excelled in the software business. It doesn't surprise me one bit because I saw that in his character. He could have pitched a fit about me, our company, American business in general, The Citadel, or the tech sector. Many noobs would have been really pissed that they had worked so hard to get such a great offer and had it pulled away. "It's not fair!" Instead, David just shrugged and said he'd deal with it. And he did.

It's those kinds of moments that define your character. People are watching, and how you react will either help you or hurt you. When I recruited David, I thought he would do very well. His response to having the job rescinded made me sure he would be successful. I wished I could have helped him transition to something new, but as it turns out, he didn't need it!

Too many noobs complain. And the reward for being a complainer is often another thing to complain about —"You're fired! Take that sulk somewhere else."

A pro (like David) expects some things not to go his way. He adjusts as he goes and expects good things to happen—and they do.

## SQUIRREL!

When I was finishing college, I networked with people in real estate to see what I could learn. I wanted to go into real estate in the Charleston area (where I went to college), which would've been a fine profession.

I sat down with one real estate pro who suggested that if it was him, he'd go to law school, major in real estate law, and become a real estate lawyer in Charleston. That way I'd get paid to be an attorney and also have the inside skinny on everything that was going on in town. He recommended that I start investing money in projects because I'd be exposed to all the real estate.

What a plan! It would have kept me in the realm I loved, close to family and friends, and with a specialty law degree. I would have a great income plus be in a great position to invest. But at the time, I couldn't hear him.

I heard his words, but I didn't really hear what he was telling me. At that age, my head was full of other things. It was crowded with school, work, my girlfriend, my friends, and basketball. That's when you get noobed. All the stuff you're reading in the business headlines about huge successes in the tech world can be the "squirrel" or shiny object that distracts you from a more rooted plan.

I had a guy tell me the smart answer. He even showed me a no-lose situation. I thought about being a lawyer. I liked Charleston and wanted to work in real estate. Everyone knew me, and my family was there. But I couldn't hear it because I wanted to chase the squirrel. Like I have said before, my life has worked out fine, but it could have been a lot easier if I'd planned it better. This doesn't mean you should never take a chance or do something out of the norm. I've told you over and over to embrace interesting opportunities!

When you're picking your first gig, follow some rough path around what you like to do. Your aptitude, training and experience-to-date, ideal location, natural contacts, anything. Try to find something in a compatible area, and you will set yourself up for a higher probability of success. In your ideal first job, how many of these natural advantages can you connect?

Think about your longer-term life plan. Ignore what's going on in your life right now for a few hours. Talk to your 30- or 40-year-old self. If you stay in the field you are choosing, what does your life look like at age 40? Are you happy dealing with the field you have chosen? Don't chase the squirrel. Chase the plan that makes the most sense.

# SWITCHING JOBS TOO OFTEN

I remember an early hire of mine who worked his way up to become a manager. At some point, even though I loved him and we had a great relationship, I told him I needed him to switch back to a sales role for the next year. I didn't have enough people in sales, but I had plenty of managers, so I thought he could do that for a year or two. He could crush the numbers and make more money.

This came as a shock to him. His head trash was that he needed to keep advancing in his career. I've learned that's not necessarily true. You don't have to move up the organization chart in a straight line. But at that moment, he believed he did.

You can be an individual contributor and get so good that you're making four times the money of a manager without the difficulty of managing eight people. And you can be left alone for the most part, other than talking to people, being friendly with them, and having business discussions around how to can help them.

That's the real goal: to uncover these ideal roles. Once you get to that point, you don't have to jump into another position right away just to feel like you're advancing. If you find the perfect fit, stick with it.

# FROM NOOB TO PRO: TWO ADVANCED CAREER GROWTH TIPS

## COMPOUND INTEREST

Remember when I said accounting is the key skill to understanding your industry? It goes for more than just sales. Accounting principles are the key to understanding your whole life.

Compound interest is one major accounting principle you need to learn. Compound interest is where your money makes interest this year, and that interest earns interest the next year, and so on, so you're earning interest on the whole total instead of the beginning sum. This eventually creates a massive snowball of wealth. According to Warren Buffet, compound interest is his basis for becoming the world's rich- est man. He has been compounding his money for a long time and, of course, picking the best places to put it to compound.

Noobs harness the principle of compound interest to grow their sales career. If a noob comes in early every day, has a great attitude, spends extra time with customers on location, does YouTube training and other certifications after hours, and makes the most calls every day, they may not see rewards immediately. You don't land the sale of a lifetime in your first couple of months.

But over time, you start to compound the interest. You might get a big sale outside the normal network you found, or the managers see your hard work and give you a promotion, or you secure a bigger or better territory. Or maybe you've been with the company for two years now, and you've done so well they're going to put you on the management track and send you to the Wharton Executive MBA Program. If a couple of things go your way—you're getting this executive MBA, and you're getting a promotion to a bigger territory— then the next thing that comes is going to be even bigger.

You're going to be more comfortable. You're going to get a deal with a Fortune 500 company. You're going to be the one they send because you hopscotched your way to the front of the line. As with anything else, as it gets better, it gets bigger. The more training you get, the more likely you are to qualify for and be sent to a bigger level of training, a better territory, a better job, or a better division.

That's the compound interest effect of following these sales tips and committing to continuous improvement in all areas that support your business skills. Your 30-year-old self will thank you for putting in the effort to compound your skill stack for 10 years! The payoff is a sure thing.

# BE YOUR OWN JORDAN

Most people spend more time learning about the details of other peoples' accomplishments than working on their own achievements.

Some people are really into a sports team and know all their statistics and performance rankings. This can be such a waste of time. They could be focusing that energy on what they are doing in their own careers. Especially with social media, it seems like so many people are following the lives of others instead of making themselves interesting.

Superstars like Michael Jordan are very much into studying and improving their own performance. His name stands for personal excellence.

So why aren't we treating ourselves like we're Jordan in whatever field we're in? Let's get a little selfish. Focus on yourself and quit spending so much time idolizing others. That is a child's game. If you are serious about being a pro, you need to take this moment to start focusing on yourself.

I knew a sales guy in Ireland in his mid-20s. He was enthusiastic, likeable, and had raw talent. I was working with his sales team, and I said, "Let's make sure we have our goals in perspective. We don't want your sales targets to be first priority in your life, but we don't want them to be on the bottom of the list either. Write down the top three-to- five priorities in your life." I shared that mine were health, family, and finances, then business and hobbies.

Everyone has a different order. Somewhere on the list will be their business/career. People put them in different places. They often forget about health, by the way—not a good plan.

This Irish guy put his favorite local soccer team as his number one. I thought he was kidding, but he was serious. I told him he had to get this under control, that family and health needed to be on the list, and to put his career before a soccer team he had nothing to do with. He refused. I'm not sure what happened to him, but his priorities were so out of whack it was impossible for him to do well at work for any length of time. If that's still his priority, I can't imagine he's doing well today. For all I know, he could be homeless in a tent outside a soccer stadium for all I know. Or perhaps he's the owner of the team by now!

As the saying goes, if you play silly games, you win silly prizes. Noobs jump around and chase lots of shiny objects, but pros get serious early on about their craft. They take steady and patient steps to get better and better over time, compounding their skill stack every year.

Be your own Jordan, and get excited about your own stats as they improve.

Go ahead—Be like Mike!

And no, "Be like Mike" doesn't mean you have to become the best basketball player ever, or a billionaire, or be super cool. Who could ever be as cool as Jordan? But you do need to become extremely focused and stay determined to be the best player ever. Do that for yourself in your field—like Mike did.

# CHAPTER 8

# WHEN IT'S TIME TO TRAIN YOUR OWN SALESPEOPLE

**M**astering sales is one thing. Teaching someone else to master sales is entirely different.

Although you could simply give this book to the salespeople you hire, manage, or train (or all three!), I'd like to share some pointers that will come in handy when it's time to lead your own sales squad, whether it's one sales intern for a summer or an entire sales team with thousands of people across dozens of territories around the world.

## Three Personnel Mistakes Noobs Make (That You Don't Have To)
### Forcing a Fit

The thing about success in sales is that it makes people want to follow you. Just like the millionaire sales experts who were all noobs once, one day you'll be a leader, too, as you make more and bigger deals. As a business owner, manager, or CEO, you'll have to find the right people for your team.

When I started using psychological profiling to test people, it was easy to figure out what those profile numbers looked like for the best salespeople. Then I could hire only people who looked like that. That made sales management simpler because I had exactly the right people. I wasn't trying to beat someone with a stick to do something they hated. Everyone was well matched to the job they were being asked to do.

Do that from the get-go. Take the time to test and get the right people. Hiring the wrong person is a bad idea for everyone. It gives them a bad taste in their mouth, which leads to poor word of mouth about you as an employer or boss. It may even lead to bad reviews online. At the very least, you'll both end up frustrated by the experience. And as the leader, you'll be leaving money on the table as your unhappy employee takes up a valuable spot in your office.

Even if it's not a mismatch of personalities, make sure the sales reps you hire have some interest in the product you're selling. You can't sell swimming pools, for example, if you're deathly afraid of water. Your salespeople need to be able to pitch the best value of your product or service. That means they need to believe it has value. If they hate what you're offering, get them out of there.

What I've learned from hiring and training is it's to the salesper- son's benefit not to work in a place where they have to be flogged to do the job. They're not happy if they're in the wrong job. Unhappy people sell low. Happy people sell high.

Make sure you've got the happiest salespeople.

## OVERLOOKING REGIONAL CONSIDERATIONS

When people just come out of school and begin looking for a job, they often apply to whatever is available that looks interesting. This is a way people get noobed. They forget to anticipate the realities of where the job is located.

For that reason, I always try to hire people from the local region. For the most part, people are going to want to work regionally, depending on where their family and friends are. A small sliver of people are going to be interested in moving nationally or globally. Not a lot of people are going to come out of Clemson and work for a shipping company in Rotterdam. Most people stay in the area where they grew up. This is normal as it is where your friends and family typically are and you have some roots.

One thing I wish I'd done sooner (and what I advise others to do) is solve the location problem early. Where do you want to be?

If I'm in Dayton, Ohio, and have a business there, I only want to hire people going to school around Dayton. I would hire people from Wright State and the University of Dayton. I wouldn't go anywhere else. The more I focus on one or two schools, the better it goes. I'll get to know their professors and career counselors; then I'll start to daisy-chain people. If I hire you and it works out, you're going to tell me about your two best friends who are juniors. It makes things easier and easier. These are all regional people.

I've learned that if I hire somebody who went to the University of Dayton but is from New Hampshire, they're probably going back to New Hampshire eventually, so I shouldn't hire them. All that invest-ment goes out the window when they disappear. That's what we learned works. If you hire people from the area who match the profile, then you build a machine. Your investments stick around.

It took me a couple of years to figure out these things, but once I did, it became easier. Of all the things I wish I'd known when I started hiring, managing and training people in sales, profiled hiring is the most important. Get the right people from a school where you know somebody who's already there. Hire people who want to work in the region. Then you can start to build a force that runs smooth. A sales machine.

Keep them happy and educated. Add a simple compensation plan, and regular weekly trainings. It's better for the comp plan to be simple than to anticipate every possible scenario. Also, it's better to be con-sistent with the training than be brilliant with it. Be steady, and never forget that getting the best reps is the most important action you will take as a sales manager.

# WASTING TIME WITH WORTHLESS MEETINGS

A morning stand-up meeting gets everybody pumped and on the same page for the day. There are several ways to do it. I set a time limit of no more than 30 minutes. The first five minutes are for chitchat, so everyone is comfortable, feels like they're part of something, and enjoys the gathering.

Then I brief them on the day. What's new? Who won the contest? How many calls are we going to make per person? What's coming up for marketing? Are we on track to meet our goals for the month? What information does the sales manager need to share?

Just make sure to do it every day at the same time, and keep it to a set time. If nothing else, it gets the day started. Whether remote or in-person, everyone has to be ready to roll at that time. I've had companies that held that first meeting at 9 a.m., 8 a.m., or even 7 a.m. The main thing is to pick a time and stick to it.

As for other meetings, how many does your team honestly need in a week to do their jobs? In a month? What about the content of those meetings? Do you need to do a fun half-hour ice breaker activity every single time you gather, or can you just get down to business and get everyone back to their desks in 20 minutes? Every minute you've got your team gathered around listening to your thoughts on holiday plans or the weather or local sports teams is time they are not selling and earning money for the company. Sure, the more social members might think it's fine to sit and gab for an hour. But your big earners will quickly grow frustrated with you eating into their productivity time.

Remember all the tasks I gave you throughout this book that you need to be doing every day? Calling, building a pipeline, researching, staying on top of relationships? Make sure you're giving your team as much office time as possible to complete those same priorities. Don't talk their ear off in pointless meetings and force them to stay late to catch up on the tasks that make them better earners.

In short: When you become a leader, stay out of your team's way. All the things you hate now, remember not to force them on your team. Give them as much time as possible to be productive, and they'll reward you with higher numbers.

## FROM NOOB TO PRO: ADVANCED PERSONNEL TIP

I've told you time and again to track various things across your sales career. Networking info, skill sets, and personal goals are three major points. This next one is crucial.

Track what your managers do that you do and don't like. Docu- ment how they get in your way. Write down how they negatively impact your sales. Take notes on all the negatives you see from leaders you work with.

The point of this is not to complain. No one likes a whiner, and I'm never going to encourage sniveling. But just like this book relies on bad examples to teach you what to do better, you can use the leaders around you as examples of what not to do.

And rather than focus only on the negative, also track what your leaders are doing well. How do your managers, VPs, and mentors encourage you to do better? What are some ways they've enhanced your selling environment? How have they made your life easier?

As you gather this information, you're really developing a roadmap to becoming the best leader you can be. By implementing the positive examples and avoiding the bad examples, you'll become a boss your sales reps love to work for. You'll build a company with the best reputation. Sales reps will crowd your door for a chance to work under you.

Collect that goldmine of knowledge as you go along. By the time you get your shot at leadership, you'll crush it and build a team of champions.

# CHAPTER 9

# LIFE AFTER NOOB

You've put in the work. You've read this entire book and digested everything I've taught you. All this knowledge and all these tips have become a part of your sales brain. You are now a selling machine.

Or you will be. Reading a book doesn't make you an expert, and one good sale doesn't make you the champ. It takes time and practice.

This entire book has prepared you to stop being a noob. You need to put in the work. Once you do, you'll change from noob to pro. Life is about change, and your sales career is no different. Expect your life to change as you include all the selling tips in this book.

So, what happens when you're no longer a noob? What does life look like? Let's talk about your next steps.

## PICKING YOUR FIRST (OR NEXT) SALES JOB

Recently I helped a young man, a junior in college, looking to get into sales. He said he'd gotten a sales internship but wanted a first job. He didn't know where to start or who he should speak with.

Side note: That's pretty much exactly where I was 30 years ago. Lots of interest, but no real guidelines for how to get there. We all start at the bottom.

I talked him through the process of where he would like to live. He thought Charleston, South Carolina, was fine. That was where he went to school, and his family was there, so it made sense.

I asked what he enjoys. He said he loves selling technology. I asked him who the top 10 technology companies are in Charleston. He knew most of them. I suggested he meet with these people. Once we narrowed down the region and the top 10 employers, it didn't take long for him to line up his first job with a great technology company in Charleston!

Finding your first job, or your next job, doesn't have to be any harder than that. When you're trying to figure out where you want to work, go in and see what they're looking for. This is such a simple piece of advice, but most people don't follow it. The vast majority of people are confused by too many choices and end up taking whatever they can get.

You need to sift your choices through a sequence of filters.

- Filter one—Preferred region
- Filter two—Your area of interest
- Filter three—Talk to the top 10 employers in the preferred location in your area of interest

Once you've got these filters in place, it's a simple matter to apply for jobs at your target companies. Apply to all 10, and you're bound to get hired by one. Then start working and put your nose to the grindstone. Make a name for yourself. And that position will become the stepping stone to your next big move.

Then keep going. Keep applying these filters. Keep growing.

## DECIDING TO BE HAPPY

Attitude is entirely your choice. All roads can lead to wherever you want—a sad road or a delightful road.

Let's say you got kicked out of school. It was a big mistake, maybe not even your fault. But it's done. You can feel happy or sad; it's your choice. No matter whose fault it was, you have a new set of choices to make. You may even end up at a better school. Now it's not looking so bad anymore. How you respond to events in life is up to you. You can find the negative or the positive in any situation. It's honestly your choice.

Stay away from people who are critical of every situation. That's the same mindset you should have when you get a "no" from a client. The sooner you figure out that life's not necessarily fair, the better off you will be. Just because something happens that appears to be bad doesn't mean it's true. You can turn it into something else.

How do you transform it into a positive? If someone ends up being a bad customer because they're hard to deal with, are high maintenance, or are slow to pay, it frees up your time to find a better customer. A "no" can also be good because you can stop your sales process and find somebody else. One major thing noobs typically do (but shouldn't) is chase down prospects forever and keep calling back to see how things are going. Really, you want to pray for a quick "no," so you can move on and find a good customer.

I'll give you a personal example. My oldest son did something stupid on campus when he was a second-semester freshman. He wrecked his Ford F-150 truck driving too fast on campus. They kicked him out of school. I thought this was a harsh penalty, but what's done is done. He called me and told me what happened. He said he'd screwed up. I asked if he had been drinking or on drugs or if anybody was hurt. He said no, it was just an honest driving mistake.

I said, "Well, we don't have a problem; we have a wrecked truck. The insurance will pay for the truck. If there's an issue with school, we'll do something different for a semester." He ended up going to Spain and traveled all over Europe, eventually learning how to speak Spanish. He came back and finished at the same school. That was a pretty good left turn. One week, he was living the normal college life, and then he was carrying a backpack through Spain. He traveled on his own from Italy, then up through Eastern Europe, and ended up in Amsterdam for two weeks.

He and I agree that getting booted from school was one of the great moments of his life so far.

In sales, the equivalent of getting kicked out of school might include not getting the job, getting fired, having your territory changed, having your comp plan changed, or being told you've lost a big account. All of these things will likely happen to you during your time in sales.

Be ready for it. Make the best of it, and remember that if you keep compounding your skills, you'll always find a way to win regardless of the company, the comp plan, or the territory. Take care of yourself, and expect the details of the game to change from time to time. If the change really stinks, switch companies. With your skill set, you have the power.

## PICKING THE BEST ROAD FOR YOU

There's a Robert Frost poem called "The Road Not Taken," which says, "Two roads diverged in a yellow wood, / And sorry I could not travel both / And be one traveler long I stood / And looked down one as far as I could."

Basically, it's about a life choice. You've got path one or path two. Path two has been less traveled. It's got some weeds on it. Not many people go down there. The purpose of the poem is to take the less traveled road because it will make all the difference.

I think that's a bunch of bullshit. Who knows where the less traveled road will lead? We don't know that it's a better road, and there are more than two roads in your life. There are so many roads you can choose. There are so many choices we can make, and they all can be full of goodness.

Another thing about the road less traveled: There could be a reason it's less traveled. It seems like an analogy, but it doesn't actually tell you any useful information. It's a cute poem, but have you ever taken a road less traveled and then ended up lost in the boonies?

If you're wondering now which road to take, let's step back. Where do you want to go from here? That brings us back to the beginning, doesn't it?

The promise of sales is freedom. Sell a lot and become financially free. Financial freedom is a career goal for many, regardless of their position or industry.

What noobs rarely do is decide at 20 how their life is going to look at 30 or 40. If you want to speak another language fluently, take a trip around the world. Have a lifelong system for managing your money, making more than you spend every month so that you snowball your net worth forward. How much of your social life do you want to be on autopilot with solid decisions? Do you want to be an expert in your space where you're earning money on sales or have your own business at some point?

This is the key to picking your road. Not looking at what other people are doing or not doing. You need to ask yourself, *Which road leads to the final destination I'm trying to reach?* Then take the route that gets you there in the strongest health.

It is very different wanting something versus deciding it's going to happen. If you do these things now, define your wants and decide to make them happen, your 50-year-old self will thank you.

The lifeline exercise is a good illustration. You estimate that you're going to reach 100 years old, draw a line from birth to age 100, and put a dot where you are now. Then write a few of the major things that have happened in your life so far. Last, make a list of the things you'd like to see, build, or experience before you hit 100. In short, you start a bucket list.

People who write down their goals find a way to get them done. On the other hand, people who wake up in the morning and do the same old thing don't succeed. And people who think about going to Egypt but don't make plans will never do it. If there's something really cool you want to do (or have a chance to do), then you need to do it. No excuses.

Do the lifeline exercise now. Draw a line on a piece of paper. List what you've done up until now and what you want to do next. What are the highlights of your future life? Write them down. Do the same for your bucket list. You will be amazed at how much more likely these things are to happen when you write them down.

# Becoming the Go-To Authority in Your Field (Whether You Stay in Sales or Not)

Noobs tend to be impatient. Plenty of them dream of becoming a thought leader in their industry, but they don't want it to take half a century.

When I think of an expert in a field, this person is 50 or 60 years old, and they've done it all. They're an instructor, or a business leader. They've written books about the knowledge they've accrued. Maybe they speak all over the world.

This is the classic example of an expert. But it doesn't take all of that to become an authority in your field. You could become a mini expert at 22 years old if you simply do the things we've talked about in this book.

Get this all-or-nothing stuff out of your mind. Don't think you're either a wise elder or a total noob. That's just more head trash. Don't wait until your Uncle Earl considers you an expert. Start now.

Begin by following everybody popular in your field on LinkedIn, Twitter, and anywhere else. Follow them, read some of their work, and comment on their social media pages. Tell them you're new in the field and think what they're doing looks interesting. By taking on their perspectives, you'll gain a new lens through which to examine your field. That's one thing I learned by training college kids: they know new stuff I don't know. My brain is full of other things. They have a unique perspective on their field, and I enjoy hearing that new perspective.

As time goes on, when you experience things that are legitimately interesting, you can put it out there for others to learn from. "Here's my first-year summary for business. Here's what I've learned about dealing with senior-level buyers." Pretty soon, you've proven yourself and started to succeed. You'll learn how to do a Twitter ladder, and more people will follow you. After a while, big names will know who you are, and they'll reply to your posts. Now you're about halfway up that ladder. If those people are talking to you, you've become a mini expert.

It's important that you don't fall for the all-or-nothing idea. Allow yourself to advance in your career on your terms at a healthy speed.

Learn to dominate your niche and be confident in what you do. One small example of this is when you're giving your elevator pitch for what you sell. Keep it simple and exciting: "I help X do Y without Z." X is your target audience, Y is the dream outcome, and Z is the biggest pain point they suffer from that you will help them avoid.

Need an example? Just look at this book. I help sales noobs become pros without making painful mistakes. And I help soon-to-be sales reps land their dream job without feeling overwhelmed.

# YOU'RE READY TO WIN

As you master all of the tips in this book, methods that have worked for so many other new sales reps, remember to keep aiming higher. Hold that vision in your mind of where you want to be someday. Keep checking in with the 30-year-old you, the 40-year-old you, and make sure they'll thank you. Revisit your lifeline diagram once a year to stay on target.

All of the sales noobs that I've mentored to pro had one thing in common: They all kept steadily improving. They continued training even as they started to master sales. They never stopped growing.

So where do you go from here? Pick your job according to the filters we've discussed. Fix your attitude. Pick the best road for your career and start walking it. Accrue experience so you can become the go-to authority in your field.

And start networking. It is never too early to begin networking in your field. You've read my book and want to be in sales, right? Look me up on LinkedIn and make the connection. You could be the next golden noob I hire and help turn pro. Or maybe we'll end up working together down the road at a company that hasn't even been created yet. The sales world can be a very small place that way.

Whatever you decide, start today. Don't wait. Build yourself and your career like you want to win, and eventually, you will.

I expect the best from you. You are on your way to the pros. I'll see you there.

# GO BEYOND THE BOOK.

Let's continue your training. Additional resources await you at www.SchoolForNoobs.com.

You'll learn to make prospects take you seriously, sell high-ticket products and services with ease, and get paid a helluva lot more than you ever did in your dreams.

# ABOUT THE AUTHOR

John Sterling is the world's foremost expert in transforming sales noobs into seasoned pros. As a sales trainer, manager, and serial entrepreneur, John is known for mentoring sales reps with zero business experience so they become high six- and seven-figure salespeople.

John built the software start-up Datastream into a publicly-traded company that sold to Infor for over $200 million. As head of Global Sales and Operations, John and his team managed acquisitions in the United Kingdom, France, Germany, Italy, Argentina, Singapore, and Australia, becoming the biggest technology company in South Carolina. During that time, John hired and trained over 150 sales reps, 60 of whom are now business owners, CEOs, or sales VPs. Currently, John is an owner and investor in technology companies in the Southern United States and consults with business owners and their sales teams to crush quota.

John captained the Citadel college basketball team, played against Michael Jordan and Magic Johnson, and played professional basketball in Ireland. After basketball, John began his sales career in Silicon Valley in computer software. On weekends, John can be found in Greenville, South Carolina, jazz clubs playing the saxophone. Take your sales team from noobs to pros at www.SchoolforNoobs.com.